Super Ea Diverticulitis Cookbook

A Beginner's Guide to Gut-Friendly Cooking with Simple to Follow Step-by-Step Instructions | 60 Day Meal Plan

Selena Newman

Copyright © 2024 By SELENA NEWMAN. All rights reserved worldwide.

No part of this book may be reproduced or transmitted in any form or by any means, electronic or mechanical, including photocopying, recording, or by any information storage and retrieval system, without written permission from the publisher, except for the inclusion of brief quotations in a review.

WARNING-DISCLAIMER:

The purpose of this book is to educate and entertain. The author or publisher does not guarantee that anyone following the techniques, suggestions, tips, ideas, or strategies will become successful. The author and publisher shall have neither liability nor responsibility to anyone with respect to any loss or damage caused, or alleged to be caused, directly or indirectly, by the information contained in this book.

This copyright notice and disclaimer apply to the entirety of the book and its contents, whether in print or electronic form, and extend to all future editions or revisions of the book. Unauthorized use or reproduction of this book or its contents is strictly prohibited and may result in legal action.

TABLE OF CONTENTS

UNDERSTANDING DIVERTICULITIS 5
GETTING STARTED WITH THE DIVERTICULITIS DIET 7
COOKING TECHNIQUES AND TIPS 9
MEAL PLANS 11
BREAKFAST RECIPES 13
    Smooth Banana Oat Porridge 14
    Spinach and Feta Frittata 14
    Berry Yoghurt Parfait 14
    Whole Grain Toast with Avocado Spread 15
    Apple Cinnamon Overnight Oats 15
    Scrambled Tofu with Herbs 15
    Peach and Ginger Smoothie Bowl 16
    Buckwheat Pancakes with Blueberry Compote 16
    Vegetable and Cheese Omelette 17
    Chia Seed Pudding with Mango 17
SOUPS AND STARTERS 18
    Creamy Butternut Squash Soup 19
    Lentil and Vegetable Broth 19
    Chilled Cucumber Gazpacho 19
    Carrot and Ginger Soup 20
    Tomato Basil Bisque 20
    Minestrone with Whole Grain Pasta 20
    Roasted Red Pepper Hummus 21
    Zucchini and Pea Soup 21
    Baked Falafel Bites 22
    Cauliflower and Potato Soup 22
MAIN COURSE: VEGETARIAN AND VEGAN 23
    Quinoa Stuffed Bell Peppers 24
    Lentil and Sweet Potato Curry 24
    Vegetable and Tofu Stir-Fry 25
    Eggplant Parmesan (Baked) 25
    Chickpea and Spinach Curry 26
    Mushroom Risotto 26
    Vegetable Lasagna with Whole Grain Pasta 27
    Black Bean and Sweet Potato Burrito Bowl 27
    Tomato and Lentil Bolognese 28
    Grilled Portobello Mushroom Steaks 28
MAIN COURSE: POULTRY AND FISH 29
    Baked Lemon Herb Chicken 30
    Grilled Salmon with Dill Sauce 30
    Turkey and Vegetable Meatloaf 30
    Poached Cod with Herb Broth 31
    Chicken and Vegetable Kebabs 31
    Baked Tilapia with Tomato and Olive Topping 31
    Turkey Burgers with Avocado Spread 32
    Baked Chicken Fajitas 32
    Tuna and White Bean Salad 32

- Lemon Garlic Roasted Chicken with Vegetables 33

SIDE DISHES 34
- Roasted Root Vegetables 35
- Quinoa Tabbouleh 35
- Steamed Green Beans with Almonds 35
- Baked Sweet Potato Wedges 36
- Sautéed Kale with Garlic 36
- Cucumber and Tomato Salad 36
- Brown Rice Pilaf 37
- Roasted Brussels Sprouts with Balsamic Glaze 37
- Mashed Cauliflower 37
- Whole Grain Couscous with Herbs 38

SMOOTHIES AND BEVERAGES 39
- Green Goddess Smoothie 40
- Berry Blast Smoothie 40
- Tropical Turmeric Smoothie 40
- Peanut Butter Banana Shake 41
- Watermelon Mint Cooler 41
- Golden Milk (Turmeric Latte) 41
- Cucumber Lemon Water 42
- Chamomile and Lavender Tea 42
- Carrot and Ginger Juice 42
- Probiotic Kefir Drink 42

SNACKS AND LIGHT BITES 43
- Baked Vegetable Crisps 44
- Homemade Granola Bars 44
- Whole Grain Crackers with Hummus 44
- Apple Slices with Almond Butter 45
- Roasted Chickpeas 45
- Greek Yogurt with Berries and Honey 45
- Vegetable Sticks with Tzatziki Dip 45
- Baked Kale Chips 46
- Whole Grain Muffins with Fruit 46
- Homemade Trail Mix 46

DESSERTS 47
- Dark Chocolate Avocado Mousse 48
- Almond and Date Energy Balls 48
- Chia Seed Pudding with Berries 48
- Banana "Nice" Cream 48
- Whole Grain Oatmeal Cookies 49
- Poached Pears in Spiced Tea 49
- Baked Apples with Cinnamon 49
- Greek Yogurt Panna Cotta 50
- Fruit Salad with Mint and Lime 50
- Berry Crumble with Oat Topping 50

GLOSSARY 51

60 DAY MEAL PLAN 53

CONCLUSION 57

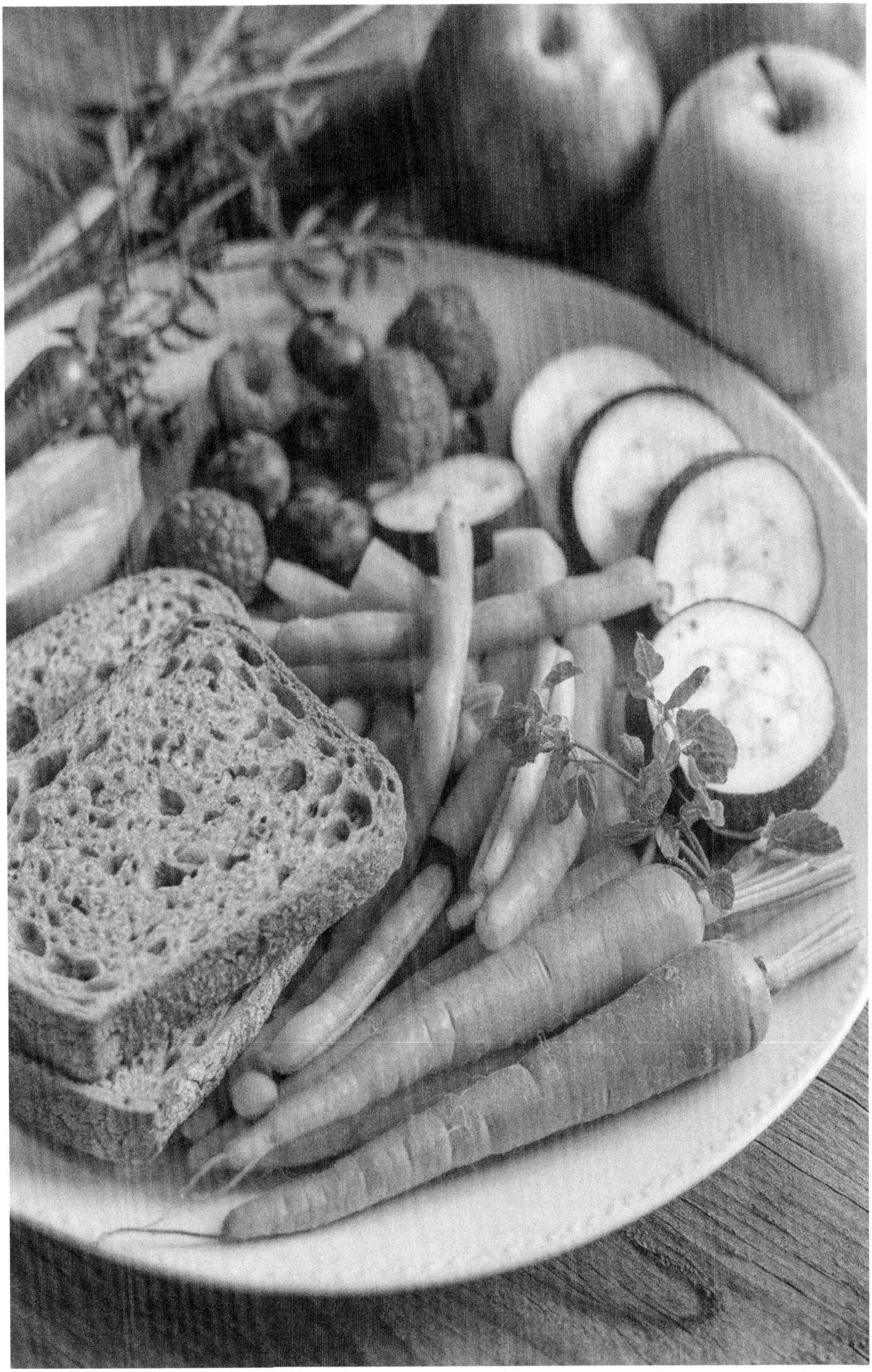

UNDERSTANDING DIVERTICULITIS

What is Diverticulitis?

When I first heard the term "diverticulitis", I was as confused as you might be right now. Let me break it down for you in simple terms. Diverticulitis is a condition that affects your digestive system, specifically your colon. It occurs when small, bulging pouches (called diverticula) that can form in the lining of your digestive system become inflamed or infected.

Imagine your colon as a smooth tube. Now, picture small pockets forming along its walls - these are diverticula. When these pockets get irritated or infected, that's diverticulitis. It can cause symptoms like abdominal pain (usually on the left side), fever, nausea, and changes in your bowel habits.

The Role of Diet in Managing Diverticulitis

Now, you might be wondering, "What's food got to do with all this?" Well, quite a lot, actually! The food we eat plays a crucial role in managing diverticulitis. In my experience, making the right dietary choices has been a game-changer in controlling my symptoms and preventing flare-ups. When you have diverticulitis, your diet becomes your first line of defence. The right foods can help reduce inflammation, promote healing, and prevent future episodes. On the flip side, certain foods might irritate your digestive system and trigger symptoms.

Diverticulitis Diet Basics

So, what should you eat? And more importantly, what should you avoid? Let's break it down:

Foods to Enjoy:

1. High-fibre foods: Once your doctor gives you the green light, gradually increase your fibre intake. Think whole grains, fruits, vegetables, and legumes. Fibre helps keep things moving smoothly through your digestive system.

2. Lean proteins: Chicken, fish, and tofu are excellent choices. They provide necessary nutrients without putting too much strain on your digestive system.

3. Probiotic-rich foods: Yoghurt, kefir, and other fermented foods can help maintain a healthy gut flora.

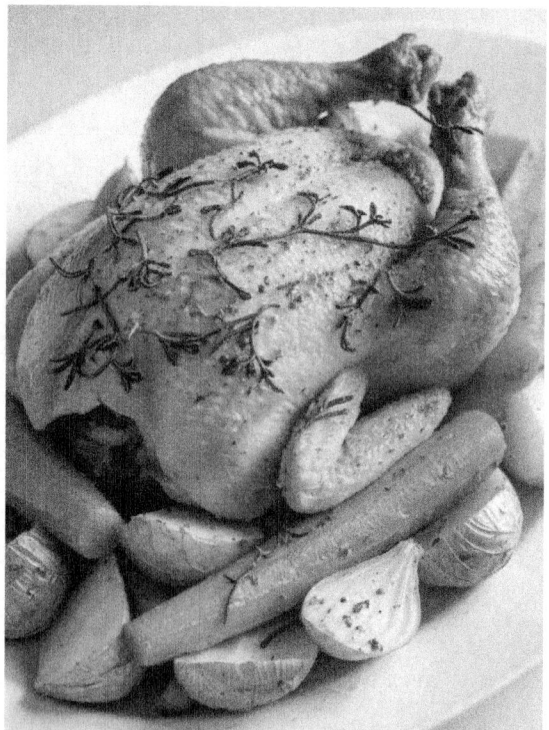

Foods to Avoid or Limit:

1. Seeds and nuts: These were once thought to be absolute no-nos, but recent research suggests they may not be as harmful as previously believed. Still, during flare-ups, it's best to avoid them.

2. Processed foods: These often lack fibre and can be hard on your digestive system.

3. Spicy foods: These can irritate your digestive tract, especially during flare-ups.

Remember, everyone's body is different. What works for me might not work exactly the same for you. It's crucial to listen to your body and work closely with your healthcare provider to find the diet that suits you best.

Nutritional Considerations

Managing diverticulitis isn't just about avoiding certain foods – it's also about ensuring you're getting the right nutrients. Here are some key considerations:

1. Fibre: Aim for 25-30 grams per day, but increase your intake gradually to avoid discomfort.

2. Hydration: Drink plenty of water. It helps fibre do its job and keeps your digestive system running smoothly.

3. Vitamins and Minerals: A balanced diet rich in fruits and vegetables will provide most of what you need. However, if you're struggling to eat a varied diet, talk to your doctor about supplements.

Understanding diverticulitis and its relationship with diet is the first step towards managing this condition effectively. In the next section, we'll dive into how to set up your kitchen and start implementing these dietary principles in your daily life.

GETTING STARTED WITH THE DIVERTICULITIS DIET

Setting Up Your Kitchen
When I first started my diverticulitis-friendly diet journey, I quickly realised that having the right tools and ingredients on hand made all the difference. Let's walk through how to set up your kitchen for success.

Essential Equipment and Tools
1. Blender or Food Processor: These are brilliant for making smoothies, soups, and purees – perfect for when you need easily digestible meals.
2. Steamer: Steaming vegetables helps retain nutrients while making them easier to digest.
3. Non-stick Pans: These allow you to cook with less oil, which can be helpful during flare-ups.
4. Slow Cooker: Brilliant for making tender, easy-to-digest meals with minimal effort.
5. Measuring Cups and Spoons: Precise measurements are key when you're trying to control your diet.

Pantry Staples for a Diverticulitis-Friendly Kitchen
Stock your pantry with these essentials:
- Whole grains (brown rice, quinoa, whole grain pasta)
- Legumes (lentils, chickpeas, beans)
- Nuts and seeds (for when you're not having a flare-up)
- Herbs and spices (for flavour without irritation)
- Low-sodium broths
- Olive oil
- Tinned fish (salmon, tuna)

Meal Planning and Preparation
Meal planning has been my secret weapon in managing diverticulitis. It helps ensure I always have suitable foods on hand, reducing the temptation to reach for less gut-friendly options.

Strategies for Successful Meal Planning
1. Plan for the Week: Take some time each weekend to plan your meals for the coming week.
2. Create a Shopping List: Based on your meal plan, make a list of everything you need. This helps avoid impulse purchases of foods that might not agree with you.
3. Prep in Batches: Spend a few hours prepping ingredients or cooking meals in batches. This can be a lifesaver on busy days.
4. Have a Backup Plan: Keep some easy, diverticulitis-friendly meals in the freezer for days when cooking feels like too much effort.

Batch Cooking and Meal Prep Tips
1. Roast Vegetables in Bulk: These can be added to salads, grain bowls, or blended into soups throughout the week.

2. Cook Large Batches of Grains: Brown rice, quinoa, or whole grain pasta can be the base for multiple meals.
3. Prepare Proteins Ahead: Grill chicken breasts or bake fish fillets to add to meals throughout the week.
4. Make Big Batches of Soup: Soups are perfect for batch cooking and freeze well.

Storage and Reheating Guidelines
- Use Airtight Containers: This keeps food fresh and prevents cross-contamination.
- Label Everything: Include the dish name and date it was prepared.
- Follow Safe Reheating Practices: Ensure food is heated thoroughly to avoid any tummy upsets.

Reading Food Labels
Learning to read food labels was a game-changer for me. It helped me make informed choices and avoid ingredients that might trigger my symptoms.

Understanding Nutrition Facts
- Fibre Content: Look for foods with higher fibre content, but remember to increase your intake gradually.
- Added Sugars: Too much sugar can upset your digestive system. Look out for hidden sugars in processed foods.
- Sodium Levels: High sodium can lead to water retention and potentially irritate your digestive tract.

Identifying Hidden Ingredients to Avoid
Watch out for:
- Artificial sweeteners
- Preservatives
- Excessive additives

These can sometimes irritate the digestive system.

Eating Out and Socialising
Having diverticulitis doesn't mean you can't enjoy a meal out or a dinner party with friends. It just requires a bit of planning and communication.

Tips for Dining Out
1. Check the Menu in Advance: Many restaurants have their menus online. Plan your meal ahead of time.
2. Don't Be Afraid to Ask Questions: Waitstaff are usually happy to help with dietary requirements.
3. Choose Simple Dishes: Grilled fish or chicken with steamed vegetables are often safe bets.
4. Be Careful with Sauces: These can sometimes contain irritating spices or high levels of fat.

Handling Social Situations and Events
1. Communicate Your Needs: Let your host know about your dietary requirements in advance.
2. Offer to Bring a Dish: This ensures there's at least one thing you can eat comfortably.
3. Eat a Small Meal Before: If you're unsure about the food options, have a small, safe meal before you go.

Travelling with Diverticulitis
Travelling with diverticulitis can be challenging, but with some preparation, it's entirely manageable.

Planning Ahead for Trips
1. Research Your Destination: Look into local cuisines and restaurants that might cater to your needs.
2. Pack Snacks: Bring along some safe, non-perishable snacks.
3. Consider Accommodation with Kitchen Facilities: This allows you to prepare your own meals if necessary.

Packing Snacks and Emergency Food
Some good options include:
- Nuts and seeds (if tolerated)
- Dried fruits
- Whole grain crackers
- Protein bars (check ingredients)

Remember, managing diverticulitis is a journey. It might take some time to figure out what works best for you, but with these strategies, you'll be well on your way to a more comfortable, symptom-free life.

COOKING TECHNIQUES AND TIPS

When I first started cooking with diverticulitis in mind, I felt a bit overwhelmed. But over time, I've discovered that with the right techniques, you can create delicious, gut-friendly meals that the whole family will enjoy. Let me share some of my favourite cooking methods and tips that have made my diverticulitis journey much more manageable and tasty!

Cooking Methods for Easy Digestion

The way you cook your food can make a big difference in how easily your body digests it. Here are some methods I've found particularly helpful:

Steaming

Steaming is a brilliant way to cook vegetables and fish. It preserves nutrients and doesn't require any added fats, making the food easier to digest. I love using a bamboo steamer for this - it gives a lovely, delicate flavour to the food.

Tip: Try steaming carrots, broccoli, and salmon together. Season with a squeeze of lemon and a sprinkle of dill for a quick, tasty meal.

Boiling and Poaching

These gentle cooking methods are perfect for when you're experiencing a flare-up or need something very easy on your digestive system.

Tip: Poached eggs on whole grain toast make for a comforting, easily digestible breakfast.

Slow Cooking

My slow cooker has been a lifesaver! It's perfect for making tender meats and vegetables that are easy to digest. Plus, the long cooking time allows flavours to develop without needing to add irritating spices.

Recipe Idea: Try a simple chicken and vegetable stew in the slow cooker. Use low-sodium broth, chicken breasts, carrots, potatoes, and a bay leaf. Cook on low for 6-8 hours for a comforting, easy-to-digest meal.

Pressure Cooking

If you're short on time, a pressure cooker can be your best friend. It can quickly cook foods until they're very tender, making them easier for your body to break down.

Tip: Use your pressure cooker to make a batch of soft, digestible brown rice. It's much quicker than on the stovetop!

Flavour Enhancement without Irritants

One of the biggest challenges I faced was making food tasty without using ingredients that might irritate my gut. Here's what I've learned:

Herb and Spice Guide

Herbs and spices can add loads of flavour without causing irritation. Some of my favourites include:

9 | Super Easy Diverticulitis Cookbook

- Basil: Great in tomato-based dishes or with chicken
- Thyme: Lovely with roasted vegetables or in soups
- Rosemary: Wonderful with roasted potatoes or grilled chicken
- Turmeric: Has anti-inflammatory properties and adds a beautiful colour to dishes
- Cinnamon: Great in oatmeal or baked goods

Tip: Start with small amounts of herbs and spices and gradually increase to find your tolerance level.

Creating Flavourful Broths and Sauces

Broths and sauces can add depth to your dishes without relying on irritating ingredients. Here's a simple recipe for a versatile vegetable broth:

1. In a large pot, combine chopped onions, carrots, celery, and garlic.
2. Add a bay leaf, a sprig of thyme, and a few peppercorns.
3. Cover with water and simmer for about an hour.
4. Strain and use as a base for soups or to cook grains.

This broth freezes well, so you can always have some on hand.

Texture Modification

During flare-ups or when you're introducing new foods, modifying the texture of your food can make it easier to digest.

Pureeing and Blending Techniques

Pureeing foods can make them easier to digest while retaining their nutritional value. Here are some tips:

1. For Smoother Soups: Use an immersion blender directly in the pot for easy blending.
2. For Fruits and Vegetables: A high-powered blender can turn almost any produce into a smooth puree.
3. Add Liquid Gradually: This helps you control the consistency of your puree.

Recipe Idea: Try a simple butternut squash soup. Roast the squash until soft, then blend with some of your homemade vegetable broth, a touch of coconut milk, and a pinch of nutmeg.

Creating Smooth Soups and Sauces

Smooth soups and sauces can be a great way to incorporate more vegetables into your diet, especially when you're having trouble with roughage.

Tip: After blending your soup or sauce, pass it through a fine-mesh strainer for an extra smooth texture.

Remember, cooking for diverticulitis doesn't mean bland, boring meals. With these techniques, you can create delicious, satisfying dishes that are kind to your gut. Don't be afraid to experiment and find what works best for you. Happy cooking!

MEAL PLANS

When I was first diagnosed with diverticulitis, the idea of meal planning seemed daunting. What could I eat? What should I avoid? How would I manage during flare-ups? Over time, I've developed a system that works well for me, and I'm excited to share it with you. Remember, these are guidelines based on my experience and general recommendations, but always consult with your healthcare provider for personalised advice.

Sample Meal Plans

I've found it helpful to have different meal plans for different stages of diverticulitis. Here, I'll share plans for three stages: acute flare-ups, recovering from flare-ups, and maintenance.

For Acute Flare-ups (Clear Liquid Diet)

During an acute flare-up, your doctor might recommend a clear liquid diet to give your digestive system a rest. This usually lasts for a few days. Here's what a day might look like:

Breakfast:
- 1 cup of herbal tea (caffeine-free)
- 1 cup of clear apple juice

Mid-morning Snack:
- 1 cup of clear vegetable broth

Lunch:
- 1 cup of clear chicken broth
- 1 bowl of lemon jelly

Afternoon Snack:
- 1 cup of clear grape juice (diluted with water)

Dinner:
- 1 cup of clear vegetable broth
- 1 cup of herbal tea

Evening Snack:
- 1 ice lolly (made from clear fruit juice)

Remember to stay hydrated throughout the day with water and clear broths.

For Recovering from Flare-ups (Low-fibre Diet)

As you start to feel better, your doctor might suggest transitioning to a low-fibre diet. This helps your digestive system continue to heal while providing more nutrients. Here's a sample day:

Breakfast:
- 2 scrambled eggs
- 1 slice of white toast with a small amount of butter
- 1 cup of herbal tea

Mid-morning Snack:
- 1 small, ripe banana

Lunch:
- Grilled chicken breast (skinless)
- 1/2 cup of cooked white rice
- 1/2 cup of cooked carrots (peeled and well-cooked)
- 1 cup of water

Afternoon Snack:
- 1 small pot of low-fat plain yoghurt
- 1 tablespoon of honey (if tolerated)

Dinner:
- Baked white fish (like cod or haddock)
- 1/2 cup of mashed potatoes (made with milk, no skin)
- 1/2 cup of cooked green beans (well-cooked)
- 1 cup of water

Evening Snack:
- 1 slice of white toast with a thin spread of smooth peanut butter

Remember, during this stage, it's important to avoid raw vegetables, fruits with seeds, whole grains, and high-fat foods. Stick to easily digestible, low-fibre options.

For Maintenance (High-fibre Diet)

Once you're feeling better and your doctor gives you the go-ahead, you can start transitioning to a high-fibre diet. This helps prevent future flare-ups. Here's what a day might look like:

11 | Super Easy Diverticulitis Cookbook

Breakfast:
- 1 cup of cooked porridge oats with a small handful of blueberries
- 1 tablespoon of ground flaxseed
- 1 cup of herbal tea or coffee (if tolerated)

Mid-morning Snack:
- 1 apple with 1 tablespoon of almond butter

Lunch:
- Wholemeal sandwich with grilled chicken, avocado, and lettuce
- 1 small pot of cherry tomatoes
- 1 pear
- Water

Afternoon Snack:
- 1 small handful of mixed nuts and dried fruit (no added sugar)
- 1 cup of green tea

Dinner:
- Grilled salmon
- 1/2 cup of quinoa
- 1 cup of roasted vegetables (e.g., broccoli, carrots, courgette)
- 1 tablespoon of olive oil (drizzled over vegetables)
- Water

Evening Snack:
- 1 small bowl of mixed berries with a dollop of Greek yoghurt

Adapting Recipes to Different Stages

One of the most valuable skills I've learned is how to adapt recipes to suit different stages of diverticulitis. Here are some tips:

1. During flare-ups:
   - Stick to clear liquids and very soft, low-fibre foods.
   - Avoid raw fruits and vegetables, whole grains, and high-fat foods.
   - Puree or blend foods to make them easier to digest.

2. Recovering from flare-ups:
   - Gradually introduce low-fibre foods.
   - Cook vegetables until very soft.
   - Choose white grains over whole grains.
   - Avoid spicy foods and limit dairy.

3. Maintenance stage:
   - Slowly increase fibre intake.
   - Introduce a variety of fruits, vegetables, and whole grains.
   - Experiment with different cooking methods.

Here's an example of how to adapt a simple chicken and vegetable dish for different stages:

Flare-up stage:
- Chicken broth with well-cooked, pureed chicken and vegetables

Recovery stage:
- Poached chicken breast with well-cooked, peeled carrots and mashed potatoes

Maintenance stage:
- Grilled chicken breast with a mixed salad and quinoa

Remember, everyone's journey with diverticulitis is different. What works for me might not work exactly the same for you. It's crucial to listen to your body, keep a food diary to track how different foods affect you, and work closely with your healthcare provider.

As you progress in your diverticulitis journey, you'll become more confident in creating meal plans and adapting recipes to suit your needs. Don't be afraid to experiment (within the guidelines provided by your doctor, of course) and find the foods and cooking methods that work best for you. With time and patience, you'll be able to enjoy a varied, delicious diet while managing your diverticulitis effectively.

BREAKFAST RECIPES

SMOOTH BANANA OAT PORRIDGE

Prep: 5 mins | Cook: 10 mins | Serves: 2

Ingredients:
- **US:** 100g rolled oats, 400ml almond milk (or milk of choice), 1 ripe banana (mashed), 1 tablespoon honey (optional), pinch of cinnamon
- **UK:** 100g rolled oats, 400ml almond milk (or milk of choice), 1 ripe banana (mashed), 1 tablespoon honey (optional), pinch of cinnamon

Instructions:
1. In a small saucepan, combine the oats and almond milk. Bring to a gentle boil over medium heat.
2. Reduce heat and let the mixture simmer for about 5-7 minutes, stirring occasionally to prevent sticking.
3. Stir in the mashed banana and cinnamon, then cook for an additional 2 minutes until the porridge is smooth and creamy.
4. If you prefer a touch of sweetness, stir in the honey.
5. Serve warm in bowls and enjoy a gut-friendly breakfast that's easy to digest and full of flavour.

Nutritional Info: Calories: 220 | Fat: 4g | Carbs: 42g | Protein: 6g

SPINACH AND FETA FRITTATA

Prep: 10 mins | Cook: 15 mins | Serves: 4

Ingredients:
- **US:** 6 eggs, 100g spinach (chopped), 100g feta cheese (crumbled), 1 tablespoon olive oil, 1 small onion (diced), salt, pepper
- **UK:** 6 eggs, 100g spinach (chopped), 100g feta cheese (crumbled), 1 tablespoon olive oil, 1 small onion (diced), salt, pepper

Instructions:
1. Preheat the oven to 180°C (350°F). Heat the olive oil in a non-stick ovenproof pan over medium heat.
2. Add the diced onion and cook for 3-4 minutes until soft and translucent.
3. Stir in the chopped spinach and cook for another 2 minutes until wilted.
4. In a separate bowl, whisk the eggs, then add the feta cheese, salt, and pepper.
5. Pour the egg mixture into the pan with the spinach and onions, ensuring an even layer.
6. Transfer the pan to the oven and bake for 10-12 minutes until the frittata is fully set.
7. Slice into wedges and serve warm for a protein-packed, tummy-friendly start to your day.

Nutritional Info: Calories: 220 | Fat: 15g | Carbs: 4g | Protein: 17g

BERRY YOGHURT PARFAIT

Prep: 5 mins | Cook: None | Serves: 2

Ingredients:
- **US:** 200g plain yoghurt (low-fat or non-dairy), 100g mixed berries (strawberries, blueberries, raspberries), 2 tablespoons honey, 30g granola
- **UK:** 200g plain yoghurt (low-fat or non-dairy), 100g mixed berries (strawberries, blueberries, raspberries), 2 tablespoons honey, 30g granola

Instructions:
1. Layer half the yoghurt in two serving glasses or bowls.
2. Add a layer of mixed berries on top.
3. Drizzle with honey, then sprinkle some granola over the berries.
4. Repeat the layering with the remaining yoghurt, berries, honey, and granola.
5. Serve immediately and enjoy a refreshing, fibre-rich breakfast that's kind to your digestion.

Nutritional Info: Calories: 180 | Fat: 5g | Carbs: 28g | Protein: 8g

WHOLE GRAIN TOAST WITH AVOCADO SPREAD

Prep: 5 mins | Cook: 2 mins | Serves: 2

Ingredients:
- **US:** 2 slices whole grain bread, 1 ripe avocado, 1 tablespoon lemon juice, salt, pepper, chilli flakes (optional)
- **UK:** 2 slices whole grain bread, 1 ripe avocado, 1 tablespoon lemon juice, salt, pepper, chilli flakes (optional)

Instructions:
1. Toast the bread slices until golden brown.
2. In a bowl, mash the avocado with the lemon juice, salt, and pepper.
3. Spread the avocado mixture evenly over the toasted bread.
4. If you like a bit of spice, sprinkle with a pinch of chilli flakes.
5. Serve immediately for a simple, nutritious breakfast that's perfect for a diverticulitis-friendly diet.

Nutritional Info: Calories: 220 | Fat: 12g | Carbs: 22g | Protein: 4g

APPLE CINNAMON OVERNIGHT OATS

Prep: 5 mins (plus overnight) | Cook: None | Serves: 2

Ingredients:
- **US:** 100g rolled oats, 250ml almond milk, 1 small apple (grated), 1 tablespoon honey, 1/2 teaspoon ground cinnamon
- **UK:** 100g rolled oats, 250ml almond milk, 1 small apple (grated), 1 tablespoon honey, 1/2 teaspoon ground cinnamon

Instructions:
1. In a jar or container, combine the oats, almond milk, grated apple, honey, and cinnamon.
2. Stir well to combine, then cover and refrigerate overnight.
3. In the morning, give the oats a good stir and enjoy cold or gently warmed.
4. A convenient, make-ahead breakfast that's full of flavour and easy on the digestive system.

Nutritional Info: Calories: 230 | Fat: 4g | Carbs: 42g | Protein: 5g

SCRAMBLED TOFU WITH HERBS

Prep: 10 mins | Cook: 10 mins | Serves: 2

Ingredients:
- **US:** 200g firm tofu (crumbled), 1 tablespoon olive oil, 1/2 teaspoon turmeric, 1 tablespoon fresh parsley (chopped), salt, pepper
- **UK:** 200g firm tofu (crumbled), 1 tablespoon olive oil, 1/2 teaspoon turmeric, 1 tablespoon fresh parsley (chopped), salt, pepper

Instructions:
1. Heat the olive oil in a non-stick pan over medium heat.
2. Add the crumbled tofu and turmeric, stirring to coat the tofu evenly in the spices.
3. Cook for 5-7 minutes, stirring occasionally, until the tofu is heated through and slightly golden.
4. Stir in the fresh parsley and season with salt and pepper.
5. Serve warm, perfect for a light, protein-rich breakfast that's gentle on the stomach.

Nutritional Info: Calories: 150 | Fat: 10g | Carbs: 3g | Protein: 12g

PEACH AND GINGER SMOOTHIE BOWL

Prep: 5 mins | Cook: None | Serves: 1

Ingredients:
- **US:** 200g frozen peaches, 100ml almond milk, 1 tablespoon fresh ginger (grated), 1 teaspoon honey, 30g granola (for topping)
- **UK:** 200g frozen peaches, 100ml almond milk, 1 tablespoon fresh ginger (grated), 1 teaspoon honey, 30g granola (for topping)

Instructions:
1. In a blender, combine the frozen peaches, almond milk, grated ginger, and honey.
2. Blend until smooth and thick, adding more milk if needed for consistency.
3. Pour the smoothie into a bowl and sprinkle with granola for added crunch.
4. Enjoy immediately for a refreshing, nutrient-packed breakfast that's easy to digest.

Nutritional Info: Calories: 200 | Fat: 3g | Carbs: 42g | Protein: 5g

BUCKWHEAT PANCAKES WITH BLUEBERRY COMPOTE

Prep: 10 mins | Cook: 15 mins | Serves: 4

Ingredients:
- **US:** 150g buckwheat flour, 1 teaspoon baking powder, 1 egg, 250ml almond milk, 100g fresh blueberries, 1 tablespoon honey, 1 tablespoon lemon juice
- **UK:** 150g buckwheat flour, 1 teaspoon baking powder, 1 egg, 250ml almond milk, 100g fresh blueberries, 1 tablespoon honey, 1 tablespoon lemon juice

Instructions:
1. In a large bowl, whisk together the buckwheat flour and baking powder.
2. In a separate bowl, beat the egg and mix it with the almond milk.
3. Pour the wet ingredients into the dry and whisk until just combined.
4. Heat a non-stick frying pan over medium heat. Pour in small amounts of the batter to form pancakes, cooking for 2-3 minutes on each side until golden.
5. Meanwhile, in a small saucepan, heat the blueberries, honey, and lemon juice over low heat, stirring occasionally, until the blueberries break down into a compote.
6. Serve the pancakes warm with the blueberry compote drizzled on top.

Nutritional Info: Calories: 220 | Fat: 6g | Carbs: 38g | Protein: 7g

VEGETABLE AND CHEESE OMELETTE

Prep: 10 mins | Cook: 10 mins | Serves: 2

Ingredients:
- **US:** 4 eggs, 50g grated cheese (cheddar or any preferred), 1 small courgette (grated), 1 small carrot (grated), 1 tablespoon olive oil, salt, pepper
- **UK:** 4 eggs, 50g grated cheese (cheddar or any preferred), 1 small courgette (grated), 1 small carrot (grated), 1 tablespoon olive oil, salt, pepper

Instructions:
1. In a bowl, whisk the eggs and season with salt and pepper.
2. Heat the olive oil in a non-stick frying pan over medium heat.
3. Add the grated courgette and carrot, cooking for 3-4 minutes until softened.
4. Pour the eggs over the vegetables, swirling the pan to ensure an even layer.
5. Sprinkle the grated cheese over the top and cook for 5-7 minutes, until the eggs are set.
6. Fold the omelette in half and slide it onto a plate. Serve immediately for a hearty, protein-rich breakfast that's easy on the digestive system.

Nutritional Info: Calories: 300 | Fat: 22g | Carbs: 5g | Protein: 21g

CHIA SEED PUDDING WITH MANGO

Prep: 5 mins (plus overnight) | Cook: None | Serves: 2

Ingredients:
- **US:** 40g chia seeds, 250ml almond milk, 1 tablespoon honey, 1 ripe mango (peeled and diced)
- **UK:** 40g chia seeds, 250ml almond milk, 1 tablespoon honey, 1 ripe mango (peeled and diced)

Instructions:
1. In a bowl, mix the chia seeds, almond milk, and honey. Stir well to prevent the chia seeds from clumping.
2. Cover and refrigerate overnight or for at least 4 hours, allowing the chia seeds to swell and form a pudding-like consistency.
3. When ready to serve, divide the chia pudding into two bowls and top with the diced mango.
4. Enjoy a light, refreshing breakfast that's full of fibre and gentle on your stomach.

Nutritional Info: Calories: 240 | Fat: 12g | Carbs: 28g | Protein: 6g

SOUPS AND STARTERS

CREAMY BUTTERNUT SQUASH SOUP

Prep: 15 mins | Cook: 25 mins | Serves: 4

Ingredients:
- **US:** 1 medium butternut squash (about 900g), 1 tablespoon olive oil, 1 small onion (chopped), 2 garlic cloves (minced), 750ml low-sodium vegetable broth, 120ml coconut milk, salt, pepper
- **UK:** 1 medium butternut squash (about 900g), 1 tablespoon olive oil, 1 small onion (chopped), 2 garlic cloves (minced), 750ml low-sodium vegetable stock, 120ml coconut milk, salt, pepper

Instructions:
1. Preheat your oven to 200°C (400°F). Peel and chop the butternut squash into cubes.
2. Toss the squash with olive oil, salt, and pepper, then roast on a baking tray for 20 minutes until soft.
3. In a large pot, sauté the chopped onion and garlic for 5 minutes until softened.
4. Add the roasted squash and vegetable broth to the pot. Bring to a boil, then simmer for 10 minutes.
5. Blend the soup using an immersion blender until smooth. Stir in the coconut milk and season to taste.
6. Serve hot with a drizzle of extra coconut milk for garnish.

Nutritional Info: Calories: 180 | Fat: 9g | Carbs: 25g | Protein: 2g

LENTIL AND VEGETABLE BROTH

Prep: 10 mins | Cook: 40 mins | Serves: 4

Ingredients:
- **US:** 1 tablespoon olive oil, 1 small onion (chopped), 2 carrots (sliced), 1 celery stalk (sliced), 100g red lentils, 1 litre low-sodium vegetable broth, 1 bay leaf, salt, pepper
- **UK:** 1 tablespoon olive oil, 1 small onion (chopped), 2 carrots (sliced), 1 celery stalk (sliced), 100g red lentils, 1 litre low-sodium vegetable stock, 1 bay leaf, salt, pepper

Instructions:
1. Heat olive oil in a large pot and sauté the onion, carrots, and celery for 5 minutes until soft.
2. Rinse the lentils and add them to the pot along with the vegetable broth and bay leaf.
3. Bring to a boil, then reduce to a simmer and cook for 30-35 minutes until the lentils are tender.
4. Remove the bay leaf and season with salt and pepper to taste before serving.

Nutritional Info: Calories: 160 | Fat: 4g | Carbs: 24g | Protein: 6g

CHILLED CUCUMBER GAZPACHO

Prep: 10 mins | Chill: 1 hour | Serves: 4

Ingredients:
- **US:** 2 large cucumbers (peeled and chopped), 250ml plain yoghurt, 2 garlic cloves (minced), 1 tablespoon olive oil, 1 tablespoon lemon juice, salt, pepper, fresh dill (for garnish)
- **UK:** 2 large cucumbers (peeled and chopped), 250ml plain yoghurt, 2 garlic cloves (minced), 1 tablespoon olive oil, 1 tablespoon lemon juice, salt, pepper, fresh dill (for garnish)

Instructions:
1. In a blender, combine the cucumbers, yoghurt, garlic, olive oil, and lemon juice. Blend until smooth.
2. Season with salt and pepper to taste.
3. Chill in the fridge for at least 1 hour before serving.
4. Garnish with fresh dill and serve cold for a refreshing starter.

Nutritional Info: Calories: 110 | Fat: 6g | Carbs: 10g | Protein: 4g

CARROT AND GINGER SOUP

Prep: 10 mins | Cook: 20 mins | Serves: 4
Ingredients:
- **US:** 500g carrots (peeled and chopped), 1 tablespoon olive oil, 1 small onion (chopped), 1 garlic clove (minced), 1 tablespoon fresh ginger (grated), 750ml low-sodium vegetable broth, salt, pepper
- **UK:** 500g carrots (peeled and chopped), 1 tablespoon olive oil, 1 small onion (chopped), 1 garlic clove (minced), 1 tablespoon fresh ginger (grated), 750ml low-sodium vegetable stock, salt, pepper

Instructions:
1. Heat olive oil in a pot and sauté the onion, garlic, and ginger for 5 minutes.
2. Add the chopped carrots and vegetable broth, then bring to a boil.
3. Reduce heat and simmer for 15-20 minutes until the carrots are tender.
4. Blend the soup until smooth using an immersion blender. Season with salt and pepper.
5. Serve hot, with a swirl of extra virgin olive oil for garnish if desired.

Nutritional Info: Calories: 130 | Fat: 5g | Carbs: 21g | Protein: 2g

TOMATO BASIL BISQUE

Prep: 10 mins | Cook: 25 mins | Serves: 4
Ingredients:
- **US:** 1 tablespoon olive oil, 1 small onion (chopped), 2 garlic cloves (minced), 800g tinned tomatoes, 500ml low-sodium vegetable broth, 100ml cream, fresh basil leaves, salt, pepper
- **UK:** 1 tablespoon olive oil, 1 small onion (chopped), 2 garlic cloves (minced), 800g tinned tomatoes, 500ml low-sodium vegetable stock, 100ml cream, fresh basil leaves, salt, pepper

Instructions:
1. Heat olive oil in a pot and sauté the onion and garlic for 5 minutes.
2. Add the tinned tomatoes and vegetable broth, and bring to a boil.
3. Reduce heat and simmer for 15 minutes, stirring occasionally.
4. Blend the soup until smooth, then stir in the cream and basil leaves. Season to taste.
5. Serve hot with fresh basil as garnish.

Nutritional Info: Calories: 180 | Fat: 10g | Carbs: 20g | Protein: 3g

MINESTRONE WITH WHOLE GRAIN PASTA

Prep: 15 mins | Cook: 30 mins | Serves: 4
Ingredients:
- **US:** 1 tablespoon olive oil, 1 small onion (chopped), 2 garlic cloves (minced), 1 carrot (chopped), 1 celery stalk (chopped), 400g tinned tomatoes, 1 litre low-sodium vegetable broth, 100g whole grain pasta, 1 courgette (chopped), 1 handful spinach, salt, pepper
- **UK:** 1 tablespoon olive oil, 1 small onion (chopped), 2 garlic cloves (minced), 1 carrot (chopped), 1 celery stalk (chopped), 400g tinned tomatoes, 1 litre low-sodium vegetable stock, 100g whole grain pasta, 1 courgette (chopped), 1 handful spinach, salt, pepper

Instructions:
1. Heat olive oil in a large pot and sauté the onion, garlic, carrot, and celery for 5 minutes.
2. Add the tinned tomatoes and vegetable broth, and bring to a boil.
3. Stir in the whole grain pasta and courgette. Simmer for 20 minutes until the pasta is cooked through.
4. Stir in the spinach and season with salt and pepper. Simmer for 2 more minutes.
5. Serve hot with a sprinkle of grated cheese if desired.

Nutritional Info: Calories: 220 | Fat: 6g | Carbs: 38g | Protein: 7g

ROASTED RED PEPPER HUMMUS

Prep: 10 mins | Cook: 20 mins | Serves: 4

Ingredients:
- **US:** 1 large red bell pepper, 1 can (400g) chickpeas (drained and rinsed), 2 tablespoons tahini, 2 tablespoons lemon juice, 1 garlic clove (minced), 2 tablespoons olive oil, 1/2 teaspoon ground cumin, salt, pepper
- **UK:** 1 large red bell pepper, 1 can (400g) chickpeas (drained and rinsed), 2 tablespoons tahini, 2 tablespoons lemon juice, 1 garlic clove (minced), 2 tablespoons olive oil, 1/2 teaspoon ground cumin, salt, pepper

Instructions:
1. Preheat the oven to 200°C (400°F). Roast the red pepper whole for 20 minutes until the skin blisters and blackens.
2. Once roasted, place the pepper in a bowl, cover, and let it steam for 5 minutes. Then, peel off the skin and remove the seeds.
3. In a blender or food processor, combine the roasted pepper, chickpeas, tahini, lemon juice, garlic, olive oil, and cumin. Blend until smooth.
4. Season with salt and pepper to taste, and serve with soft pita or vegetable sticks.

Nutritional Info: Calories: 150 | Fat: 8g | Carbs: 15g | Protein: 4g

ZUCCHINI AND PEA SOUP

Prep: 10 mins | Cook: 20 mins | Serves: 4

Ingredients:
- **US:** 1 tablespoon olive oil, 1 small onion (chopped), 2 garlic cloves (minced), 3 medium zucchinis (chopped), 200g frozen peas, 750ml low-sodium vegetable broth, 1 tablespoon lemon juice, salt, pepper, fresh mint leaves (for garnish)
- **UK:** 1 tablespoon olive oil, 1 small onion (chopped), 2 garlic cloves (minced), 3 medium courgettes (chopped), 200g frozen peas, 750ml low-sodium vegetable stock, 1 tablespoon lemon juice, salt, pepper, fresh mint leaves (for garnish)

Instructions:
1. Heat olive oil in a large pot and sauté the onion and garlic for 5 minutes.
2. Add the chopped zucchinis (courgettes) and cook for 5 more minutes.
3. Pour in the vegetable broth and add the peas. Bring to a boil, then reduce to a simmer and cook for 10 minutes.
4. Blend the soup until smooth, then stir in the lemon juice. Season with salt and pepper to taste.
5. Serve hot, garnished with fresh mint leaves.

Nutritional Info: Calories: 120 | Fat: 5g | Carbs: 18g | Protein: 4g

BAKED FALAFEL BITES

Prep: 15 mins | Cook: 25 mins | Serves: 4
Ingredients:
- **US:** 1 can (400g) chickpeas (drained and rinsed), 1 small onion (chopped), 2 garlic cloves (minced), 1 tablespoon olive oil, 2 tablespoons chopped fresh parsley, 1 tablespoon lemon juice, 1 teaspoon ground cumin, 1 teaspoon ground coriander, 1 tablespoon flour, salt, pepper
- **UK:** 1 can (400g) chickpeas (drained and rinsed), 1 small onion (chopped), 2 garlic cloves (minced), 1 tablespoon olive oil, 2 tablespoons chopped fresh parsley, 1 tablespoon lemon juice, 1 teaspoon ground cumin, 1 teaspoon ground coriander, 1 tablespoon flour, salt, pepper

Instructions:
1. Preheat the oven to 200°C (400°F) and line a baking tray with parchment paper.
2. In a food processor, combine the chickpeas, onion, garlic, parsley, lemon juice, cumin, coriander, and flour. Pulse until it forms a coarse mixture.
3. Shape the mixture into small balls or patties and place them on the prepared tray.
4. Drizzle with olive oil and bake for 20-25 minutes, flipping halfway through, until golden and crispy.
5. Serve with a side of tahini sauce or yoghurt dip.

Nutritional Info: Calories: 180 | Fat: 7g | Carbs: 25g | Protein: 6g

CAULIFLOWER AND POTATO SOUP

Prep: 10 mins | Cook: 25 mins | Serves: 4
Ingredients:
- **US:** 1 tablespoon olive oil, 1 small onion (chopped), 2 garlic cloves (minced), 1 medium cauliflower (chopped), 2 medium potatoes (peeled and diced), 750ml low-sodium vegetable broth, 120ml milk, salt, pepper
- **UK:** 1 tablespoon olive oil, 1 small onion (chopped), 2 garlic cloves (minced), 1 medium cauliflower (chopped), 2 medium potatoes (peeled and diced), 750ml low-sodium vegetable stock, 120ml milk, salt, pepper

Instructions:
1. Heat olive oil in a large pot and sauté the onion and garlic for 5 minutes.
2. Add the chopped cauliflower and diced potatoes, and cook for another 5 minutes.
3. Pour in the vegetable broth and bring to a boil. Reduce to a simmer and cook for 20 minutes until the vegetables are soft.
4. Blend the soup until smooth using an immersion blender. Stir in the milk and season with salt and pepper.
5. Serve hot, garnished with fresh parsley or a drizzle of olive oil if desired.

Nutritional Info: Calories: 150 | Fat: 6g | Carbs: 22g | Protein: 3g

MAIN COURSE: VEGETARIAN AND VEGAN

QUINOA STUFFED BELL PEPPERS

Prep: 15 mins | Cook: 30 mins | Serves: 4

Ingredients:
- **US:** 4 bell peppers, 150g quinoa, 240ml vegetable broth, 1 small onion (finely chopped), 2 garlic cloves (minced), 1 teaspoon olive oil, 1 teaspoon dried oregano, salt, pepper, 2 tablespoons fresh parsley (chopped)
- **UK:** 4 bell peppers, 150g quinoa, 240ml vegetable stock, 1 small onion (finely chopped), 2 garlic cloves (minced), 1 teaspoon olive oil, 1 teaspoon dried oregano, salt, pepper, 2 tablespoons fresh parsley (chopped)

Instructions:
1. Preheat your oven to 180°C (350°F).
2. Cut the tops off the bell peppers and remove the seeds and membranes inside. Set the peppers aside.
3. Cook the quinoa in the vegetable broth according to package instructions.
4. In a pan, heat olive oil over medium heat and sauté the onions and garlic for 3-4 minutes, until softened.
5. Add the cooked quinoa, oregano, salt, and pepper. Stir well.
6. Stuff each bell pepper with the quinoa mixture, place them in a baking dish, and cover with foil.
7. Bake for 25-30 minutes until the peppers are tender.
8. Garnish with fresh parsley before serving.

Nutritional Info: Calories: 200 | Fat: 5g | Carbs: 35g | Protein: 6g

LENTIL AND SWEET POTATO CURRY

Prep: 10 mins | Cook: 40 mins | Serves: 4

Ingredients:
- **US:** 200g red lentils, 1 large sweet potato (diced), 1 onion (chopped), 3 garlic cloves (minced), 400ml coconut milk, 400g canned tomatoes, 1 tablespoon curry powder, 1 teaspoon cumin, 1 teaspoon turmeric, salt, pepper, 1 tablespoon olive oil, 2 tablespoons fresh coriander (chopped)
- **UK:** 200g red lentils, 1 large sweet potato (diced), 1 onion (chopped), 3 garlic cloves (minced), 400ml coconut milk, 400g tinned tomatoes, 1 tablespoon curry powder, 1 teaspoon cumin, 1 teaspoon turmeric, salt, pepper, 1 tablespoon olive oil, 2 tablespoons fresh coriander (chopped)

Instructions:
1. Heat the olive oil in a large pot over medium heat. Add the onion and garlic and sauté for 5 minutes.
2. Stir in the curry powder, cumin, and turmeric and cook for another minute.
3. Add the sweet potato, lentils, coconut milk, and tomatoes. Bring the mixture to a boil.
4. Reduce heat, cover, and simmer for 30-35 minutes, stirring occasionally, until the lentils and sweet potatoes are tender.
5. Season with salt and pepper to taste.
6. Serve hot, garnished with fresh coriander.

Nutritional Info: Calories: 350 | Fat: 14g | Carbs: 45g | Protein: 11g

VEGETABLE AND TOFU STIR-FRY

Prep: 10 mins | Cook: 15 mins | Serves: 4

Ingredients:
- **US:** 400g tofu (cubed), 1 red bell pepper (sliced), 1 courgette (sliced), 1 carrot (julienned), 2 tablespoons soy sauce, 1 tablespoon sesame oil, 1 garlic clove (minced), 1 teaspoon grated ginger, sesame seeds (for garnish)
- **UK:** 400g tofu (cubed), 1 red pepper (sliced), 1 courgette (sliced), 1 carrot (julienned), 2 tablespoons soy sauce, 1 tablespoon sesame oil, 1 garlic clove (minced), 1 teaspoon grated ginger, sesame seeds (for garnish)

Instructions:
1. Heat the sesame oil in a wok or large frying pan over medium-high heat.
2. Add the garlic and ginger, and cook for 1 minute until fragrant.
3. Add the tofu and stir-fry for 5 minutes until golden brown.
4. Toss in the vegetables and stir-fry for another 5-7 minutes until tender but still crisp.
5. Stir in the soy sauce and cook for 1 minute more.
6. Serve hot, garnished with sesame seeds.

Nutritional Info: Calories: 280 | Fat: 18g | Carbs: 16g | Protein: 14g

EGGPLANT PARMESAN (BAKED)

Prep: 20 mins | Cook: 45 mins | Serves: 4

Ingredients:
- **US:** 2 medium eggplants, 200g breadcrumbs, 50g grated parmesan, 1 teaspoon dried oregano, 2 eggs (beaten), 400g canned tomatoes, 100g mozzarella (sliced), 1 tablespoon olive oil
- **UK:** 2 medium aubergines, 200g breadcrumbs, 50g grated parmesan, 1 teaspoon dried oregano, 2 eggs (beaten), 400g tinned tomatoes, 100g mozzarella (sliced), 1 tablespoon olive oil

Instructions:
1. Preheat the oven to 200°C (400°F). Slice the eggplants into 1cm rounds.
2. Dip each slice into the beaten eggs, then coat with a mixture of breadcrumbs, parmesan, and oregano.
3. Arrange the slices on a baking sheet and drizzle with olive oil. Bake for 20 minutes until golden.
4. In a baking dish, layer the eggplant slices, tomatoes, and mozzarella.
5. Bake for an additional 25 minutes until bubbly and golden on top.

Nutritional Info: Calories: 320 | Fat: 16g | Carbs: 35g | Protein: 15g

CHICKPEA AND SPINACH CURRY

Prep: 10 mins | Cook: 20 mins | Serves: 4

Ingredients:
- **US:** 400g canned chickpeas (drained), 200g fresh spinach, 1 onion (chopped), 2 garlic cloves (minced), 1 tablespoon curry powder, 400g canned tomatoes, 200ml coconut milk, 1 tablespoon olive oil, salt, pepper
- **UK:** 400g tinned chickpeas (drained), 200g fresh spinach, 1 onion (chopped), 2 garlic cloves (minced), 1 tablespoon curry powder, 400g tinned tomatoes, 200ml coconut milk, 1 tablespoon olive oil, salt, pepper

Instructions:
1. Heat the olive oil in a large pan over medium heat. Add the onions and garlic, and sauté for 5 minutes.
2. Stir in the curry powder and cook for 1 minute.
3. Add the chickpeas, tomatoes, and coconut milk, and simmer for 10 minutes.
4. Add the spinach and cook for another 5 minutes until wilted.
5. Season with salt and pepper to taste.

Nutritional Info: Calories: 250 | Fat: 12g | Carbs: 30g | Protein: 7g

MUSHROOM RISOTTO

Prep: 10 mins | Cook: 25 mins | Serves: 4

Ingredients:
- **US:** 300g Arborio rice, 200g mushrooms (sliced), 1 small onion (chopped), 2 garlic cloves (minced), 1 tablespoon olive oil, 120ml white wine (optional), 1 litre vegetable broth, 50g parmesan (grated), 2 tablespoons fresh parsley (chopped), salt, pepper
- **UK:** 300g Arborio rice, 200g mushrooms (sliced), 1 small onion (chopped), 2 garlic cloves (minced), 1 tablespoon olive oil, 120ml white wine (optional), 1 litre vegetable stock, 50g parmesan (grated), 2 tablespoons fresh parsley (chopped), salt, pepper

Instructions:
1. Heat the olive oil in a large pan over medium heat. Sauté the onions and garlic for 5 minutes until softened.
2. Add the mushrooms and cook for 5 minutes until browned.
3. Stir in the Arborio rice and cook for 1-2 minutes, allowing it to absorb the flavours.
4. If using, add the wine and cook until mostly evaporated.
5. Gradually add the vegetable broth, one ladleful at a time, stirring continuously. Wait until most of the liquid is absorbed before adding more broth.
6. Once the rice is creamy and tender (after about 20 minutes), stir in the parmesan, salt, and pepper.
7. Garnish with parsley and serve hot.

Nutritional Info: Calories: 380 | Fat: 12g | Carbs: 60g | Protein: 9g

VEGETABLE LASAGNA WITH WHOLE GRAIN PASTA

Prep: 20 mins | Cook: 45 mins | Serves: 6

Ingredients:
- **US:** 12 whole grain lasagna noodles, 500g spinach (fresh or frozen), 200g ricotta cheese, 1 egg (beaten), 500g marinara sauce, 200g mozzarella (shredded), 50g parmesan (grated), salt, pepper, 1 teaspoon olive oil
- **UK:** 12 whole grain lasagna sheets, 500g spinach (fresh or frozen), 200g ricotta cheese, 1 egg (beaten), 500g tomato sauce, 200g mozzarella (grated), 50g parmesan (grated), salt, pepper, 1 teaspoon olive oil

Instructions:
1. Preheat your oven to 180°C (350°F).
2. Boil the lasagna noodles according to package instructions. Drain and set aside.
3. In a bowl, mix the ricotta cheese, beaten egg, spinach, salt, and pepper.
4. Spread a thin layer of marinara sauce at the bottom of a baking dish.
5. Layer lasagna noodles, ricotta mixture, marinara sauce, and mozzarella. Repeat the layers, ending with mozzarella on top.
6. Sprinkle with parmesan and bake for 35-40 minutes until golden and bubbling.
7. Let the lasagna cool for 10 minutes before slicing and serving.

Nutritional Info: Calories: 420 | Fat: 18g | Carbs: 45g | Protein: 20g

BLACK BEAN AND SWEET POTATO BURRITO BOWL

Prep: 15 mins | Cook: 25 mins | Serves: 4

Ingredients:
- **US:** 400g canned black beans (drained), 2 medium sweet potatoes (cubed), 200g cooked brown rice, 1 avocado (sliced), 100g corn (cooked), 2 tablespoons olive oil, 1 teaspoon cumin, 1 teaspoon smoked paprika, salt, pepper, fresh coriander (for garnish)
- **UK:** 400g tinned black beans (drained), 2 medium sweet potatoes (cubed), 200g cooked brown rice, 1 avocado (sliced), 100g sweetcorn (cooked), 2 tablespoons olive oil, 1 teaspoon cumin, 1 teaspoon smoked paprika, salt, pepper, fresh coriander (for garnish)

Instructions:
1. Preheat the oven to 200°C (400°F). Toss the sweet potatoes in olive oil, cumin, paprika, salt, and pepper, and roast for 20-25 minutes until tender.
2. In a bowl, combine the cooked rice, black beans, corn, and roasted sweet potatoes.
3. Top with sliced avocado and garnish with fresh coriander.
4. Serve the burrito bowls warm, or store them in the fridge for an easy meal prep option.

Nutritional Info: Calories: 450 | Fat: 18g | Carbs: 65g | Protein: 12g

TOMATO AND LENTIL BOLOGNESE

Prep: 10 mins | Cook: 30 mins | Serves: 4

Ingredients:
- **US:** 200g red lentils, 1 onion (chopped), 2 garlic cloves (minced), 400g canned tomatoes, 2 tablespoons tomato paste, 1 tablespoon olive oil, 1 teaspoon dried basil, 1 teaspoon dried oregano, salt, pepper, 400g whole wheat pasta (cooked)
- **UK:** 200g red lentils, 1 onion (chopped), 2 garlic cloves (minced), 400g tinned tomatoes, 2 tablespoons tomato purée, 1 tablespoon olive oil, 1 teaspoon dried basil, 1 teaspoon dried oregano, salt, pepper, 400g whole wheat pasta (cooked)

Instructions:
1. Heat the olive oil in a large pan over medium heat. Sauté the onion and garlic for 5 minutes.
2. Add the tomato paste, tomatoes, and lentils. Stir well and bring to a simmer.
3. Add the dried basil and oregano, and cook for 25-30 minutes, until the lentils are soft and the sauce has thickened.
4. Season with salt and pepper.
5. Serve the bolognese over cooked whole wheat pasta.

Nutritional Info: Calories: 390 | Fat: 9g | Carbs: 65g | Protein: 18g

GRILLED PORTOBELLO MUSHROOM STEAKS

Prep: 5 mins | Cook: 15 mins | Serves: 4

Ingredients:
- **US:** 4 large portobello mushrooms, 2 tablespoons balsamic vinegar, 1 tablespoon olive oil, 1 teaspoon soy sauce, 1 teaspoon garlic powder, salt, pepper, fresh thyme (for garnish)
- **UK:** 4 large portobello mushrooms, 2 tablespoons balsamic vinegar, 1 tablespoon olive oil, 1 teaspoon soy sauce, 1 teaspoon garlic powder, salt, pepper, fresh thyme (for garnish)

Instructions:
1. Preheat your grill or grill pan to medium-high heat.
2. In a small bowl, mix together the balsamic vinegar, olive oil, soy sauce, garlic powder, salt, and pepper.
3. Brush the mushrooms with the marinade, coating both sides.
4. Grill the mushrooms for 5-7 minutes on each side, until they are tender and slightly charred.
5. Garnish with fresh thyme and serve hot.

Nutritional Info: Calories: 120 | Fat: 7g | Carbs: 10g | Protein: 4g

MAIN COURSE: POULTRY AND FISH

BAKED LEMON HERB CHICKEN

Prep: 10 mins | Cook: 30 mins | Serves: 4

Ingredients:
- **US:** 4 boneless, skinless chicken breasts (about 150g each), 60ml olive oil, 2 tablespoons fresh lemon juice, 2 teaspoons dried oregano, 1 garlic clove (minced), salt and pepper (to taste), fresh parsley (for garnish)
- **UK:** 4 boneless, skinless chicken breasts (about 150g each), 60ml olive oil, 2 tablespoons fresh lemon juice, 2 teaspoons dried oregano, 1 garlic clove (minced), salt and pepper (to taste), fresh parsley (for garnish)

Instructions:
1. Preheat your oven to 200°C (400°F).
2. In a bowl, mix olive oil, lemon juice, oregano, garlic, salt, and pepper.
3. Rub the mixture all over the chicken breasts and place them in a baking dish.
4. Bake for 25-30 minutes until the chicken is cooked through and the juices run clear.
5. Garnish with fresh parsley before serving.

Nutritional Info: Calories: 280 | Fat: 14g | Carbs: 3g | Protein: 36g

GRILLED SALMON WITH DILL SAUCE

Prep: 5 mins | Cook: 10 mins | Serves: 2

Ingredients:
- **US:** 2 salmon fillets (about 180g each), 1 tablespoon olive oil, 1 tablespoon lemon juice, salt and pepper (to taste), 60g Greek yoghurt, 1 tablespoon fresh dill (chopped)
- **UK:** 2 salmon fillets (about 180g each), 1 tablespoon olive oil, 1 tablespoon lemon juice, salt and pepper (to taste), 60g Greek yoghurt, 1 tablespoon fresh dill (chopped)

Instructions:
1. Preheat the grill to medium-high heat.
2. Rub the salmon with olive oil, lemon juice, salt, and pepper.
3. Grill the salmon for 4-5 minutes per side until fully cooked.
4. Meanwhile, mix the yoghurt and dill to make the sauce.
5. Serve the salmon with a dollop of dill sauce on top.

Nutritional Info: Calories: 360 | Fat: 24g | Carbs: 2g | Protein: 35g

TURKEY AND VEGETABLE MEATLOAF

Prep: 15 mins | Cook: 1 hour | Serves: 6

Ingredients:
- **US:** 500g ground turkey, 1 egg, 1 small onion (chopped), 1 carrot (grated), 1 zucchini (grated), 50g breadcrumbs, 2 tablespoons tomato paste, salt and pepper (to taste)
- **UK:** 500g ground turkey, 1 egg, 1 small onion (chopped), 1 carrot (grated), 1 courgette (grated), 50g breadcrumbs, 2 tablespoons tomato purée, salt and pepper (to taste)

Instructions:
1. Preheat your oven to 180°C (350°F).
2. In a large bowl, mix turkey, egg, onion, carrot, zucchini, breadcrumbs, and tomato paste. Season with salt and pepper.
3. Press the mixture into a loaf tin and bake for 1 hour or until cooked through.
4. Let it rest for 10 minutes before slicing.

Nutritional Info: Calories: 220 | Fat: 10g | Carbs: 10g | Protein: 25g

POACHED COD WITH HERB BROTH

Prep: 5 mins | Cook: 15 mins | Serves: 2

Ingredients:
- **US:** 2 cod fillets (about 150g each), 500ml vegetable stock, 1 tablespoon fresh parsley (chopped), 1 teaspoon fresh thyme, salt and pepper (to taste), 1 lemon (sliced)
- **UK:** 2 cod fillets (about 150g each), 500ml vegetable stock, 1 tablespoon fresh parsley (chopped), 1 teaspoon fresh thyme, salt and pepper (to taste), 1 lemon (sliced)

Instructions:
1. In a deep pan, bring the vegetable stock to a simmer.
2. Add the cod fillets, thyme, parsley, salt, and pepper.
3. Poach the fish for 10-12 minutes, until it flakes easily with a fork.
4. Serve with lemon slices on top.

Nutritional Info: Calories: 160 | Fat: 2g | Carbs: 4g | Protein: 32g

CHICKEN AND VEGETABLE KEBABS

Prep: 15 mins | Cook: 15 mins | Serves: 4

Ingredients:
- **US:** 400g chicken breast (cut into cubes), 1 red bell pepper, 1 zucchini, 1 onion, 2 tablespoons olive oil, 1 teaspoon paprika, salt and pepper (to taste)
- **UK:** 400g chicken breast (cut into cubes), 1 red bell pepper, 1 courgette, 1 onion, 2 tablespoons olive oil, 1 teaspoon paprika, salt and pepper (to taste)

Instructions:
1. Preheat the grill to medium heat.
2. Thread chicken, pepper, zucchini, and onion onto skewers.
3. Brush the kebabs with olive oil and season with paprika, salt, and pepper.
4. Grill the kebabs for 12-15 minutes, turning occasionally until cooked through.

Nutritional Info: Calories: 220 | Fat: 10g | Carbs: 6g | Protein: 27g

BAKED TILAPIA WITH TOMATO AND OLIVE TOPPING

Prep: 10 mins | Cook: 20 mins | Serves: 2

Ingredients:
- **US:** 2 tilapia fillets (about 150g each), 2 tomatoes (chopped), 30g black olives (sliced), 1 garlic clove (minced), 1 tablespoon olive oil, salt and pepper (to taste)
- **UK:** 2 tilapia fillets (about 150g each), 2 tomatoes (chopped), 30g black olives (sliced), 1 garlic clove (minced), 1 tablespoon olive oil, salt and pepper (to taste)

Instructions:
1. Preheat your oven to 180°C (350°F).
2. In a bowl, mix tomatoes, olives, garlic, olive oil, salt, and pepper.
3. Place the tilapia fillets in a baking dish and top with the tomato mixture.
4. Bake for 15-20 minutes until the fish flakes easily.

Nutritional Info: Calories: 200 | Fat: 10g | Carbs: 6g | Protein: 24g

TURKEY BURGERS WITH AVOCADO SPREAD

Prep: 10 mins | Cook: 15 mins | Serves: 4

Ingredients:
- **US:** 400g ground turkey, 1 egg, 50g breadcrumbs, 1 avocado (mashed), 1 tablespoon lemon juice, 1 teaspoon garlic powder, salt and pepper (to taste)
- **UK:** 400g ground turkey, 1 egg, 50g breadcrumbs, 1 avocado (mashed), 1 tablespoon lemon juice, 1 teaspoon garlic powder, salt and pepper (to taste)

Instructions:
1. In a bowl, mix ground turkey, egg, breadcrumbs, garlic powder, salt, and pepper.
2. Form into 4 patties and grill for 5-6 minutes per side.
3. Mash the avocado with lemon juice and serve the burgers with the avocado spread on top.

Nutritional Info: Calories: 310 | Fat: 18g | Carbs: 12g | Protein: 25g

BAKED CHICKEN FAJITAS

Prep: 10 mins | Cook: 25 mins | Serves: 4

Ingredients:
- **US:** 400g chicken breast (sliced), 1 red bell pepper, 1 yellow bell pepper, 1 onion, 2 tablespoons olive oil, 1 teaspoon cumin, 1 teaspoon paprika, salt and pepper (to taste)
- **UK:** 400g chicken breast (sliced), 1 red bell pepper, 1 yellow bell pepper, 1 onion, 2 tablespoons olive oil, 1 teaspoon cumin, 1 teaspoon paprika, salt and pepper (to taste)

Instructions:
1. Preheat your oven to 200°C (400°F).
2. In a bowl, toss chicken, peppers, onion, olive oil, cumin, paprika, salt, and pepper.
3. Spread the mixture on a baking tray and bake for 25 minutes.
4. Serve with tortillas if tolerated.

Nutritional Info: Calories: 280 | Fat: 12g | Carbs: 10g | Protein: 30g

TUNA AND WHITE BEAN SALAD

Prep: 5 mins | Cook: 0 mins | Serves: 2

Ingredients:
- **US:** 1 can tuna (drained), 200g white beans (canned, drained), 1 tablespoon olive oil, 1 tablespoon lemon juice, salt and pepper (to taste), fresh parsley (chopped)
- **UK:** 1 can tuna (drained), 200g white beans (canned, drained), 1 tablespoon olive oil, 1 tablespoon lemon juice, salt and pepper (to taste), fresh parsley (chopped)

Instructions:
1. In a bowl, combine tuna, white beans, olive oil, lemon juice, salt, and pepper.
2. Toss well and garnish with fresh parsley.

Nutritional Info: Calories: 250 | Fat: 8g | Carbs: 22g | Protein: 25g

LEMON GARLIC ROASTED CHICKEN WITH VEGETABLES

Prep: 15 mins | Cook: 45 mins | Serves: 4

Ingredients:
- **US:** 4 chicken thighs (bone-in, skin-on), 2 tablespoons olive oil, 2 garlic cloves (minced), 1 lemon (sliced), 2 carrots (sliced), 2 potatoes (cubed), salt and pepper (to taste)
- **UK:** 4 chicken thighs (bone-in, skin-on), 2 tablespoons olive oil, 2 garlic cloves (minced), 1 lemon (sliced), 2 carrots (sliced), 2 potatoes (cubed), salt and pepper (to taste)

Instructions:
1. Preheat your oven to 200°C (400°F).
2. In a bowl, toss chicken thighs with olive oil, garlic, lemon slices, salt, and pepper.
3. Spread the chicken and vegetables on a baking tray and roast for 40-45 minutes.
4. Serve with a squeeze of lemon over the chicken.

Nutritional Info: Calories: 450 | Fat: 25g | Carbs: 20g | Protein: 35g

SIDE DISHES

ROASTED ROOT VEGETABLES

Prep: 10 mins | Cook: 35 mins | Serves: 4

Ingredients:
- **US:** 500g carrots (peeled and cut into chunks), 500g parsnips (peeled and cut into chunks), 30ml olive oil, 1 tsp dried thyme, 1 tsp dried rosemary, Salt and pepper to taste
- **UK:** 500g carrots (peeled and cut into chunks), 500g parsnips (peeled and cut into chunks), 30ml olive oil, 1 tsp dried thyme, 1 tsp dried rosemary, Salt and pepper to taste

Instructions:
1. Preheat your oven to 200°C (180°C fan)/400°F.
2. Toss the carrot and parsnip chunks in olive oil, thyme, rosemary, salt, and pepper until evenly coated.
3. Spread the vegetables in a single layer on a baking tray.
4. Roast for 30-35 minutes, turning halfway through, until they are tender and caramelised.
5. Serve warm as a hearty side dish.

Nutritional Info: Calories: 200 | Fat: 10g | Carbs: 28g | Protein: 2g

QUINOA TABBOULEH

Prep: 15 mins | Cook: 15 mins | Serves: 4

Ingredients:
- **US:** 200g quinoa, 300ml water, 100g cherry tomatoes (diced), 100g cucumber (diced), 30g fresh parsley (chopped), 30ml lemon juice, 30ml olive oil, Salt and pepper to taste
- **UK:** 200g quinoa, 300ml water, 100g cherry tomatoes (diced), 100g cucumber (diced), 30g fresh parsley (chopped), 30ml lemon juice, 30ml olive oil, Salt and pepper to taste

Instructions:
1. Rinse quinoa under cold water. In a pot, bring 300ml water to a boil, add quinoa, and simmer for 15 minutes until cooked.
2. Fluff the quinoa with a fork and let it cool.
3. In a large bowl, combine the cooled quinoa, cherry tomatoes, cucumber, and parsley.
4. Drizzle with lemon juice and olive oil, and season with salt and pepper.
5. Mix well and serve chilled or at room temperature.

Nutritional Info: Calories: 180 | Fat: 8g | Carbs: 22g | Protein: 6g

STEAMED GREEN BEANS WITH ALMONDS

Prep: 10 mins | Cook: 10 mins | Serves: 4

Ingredients:
- **US:** 300g green beans (trimmed), 30g sliced almonds, 15ml olive oil, 1 clove garlic (minced), Salt and pepper to taste
- **UK:** 300g green beans (trimmed), 30g sliced almonds, 15ml olive oil, 1 clove garlic (minced), Salt and pepper to taste

Instructions:
1. Steam the green beans for 5-7 minutes until tender-crisp.
2. In a small pan, heat olive oil and sauté garlic until fragrant.
3. Add sliced almonds and cook for 2 minutes until lightly toasted.
4. Toss the green beans with the garlic-almond mixture.
5. Season with salt and pepper, and serve warm.

Nutritional Info: Calories: 130 | Fat: 9g | Carbs: 8g | Protein: 4g

BAKED SWEET POTATO WEDGES

Prep: 10 mins | Cook: 25 mins | Serves: 4

Ingredients:
- **US:** 500g sweet potatoes (peeled and cut into wedges), 30ml olive oil, 1 tsp smoked paprika, 1 tsp garlic powder, Salt and pepper to taste
- **UK:** 500g sweet potatoes (peeled and cut into wedges), 30ml olive oil, 1 tsp smoked paprika, 1 tsp garlic powder, Salt and pepper to taste

Instructions:
1. Preheat your oven to 220°C (200°C fan)/425°F.
2. Toss sweet potato wedges in olive oil, smoked paprika, garlic powder, salt, and pepper.
3. Spread in a single layer on a baking tray.
4. Bake for 20-25 minutes, turning halfway through, until crispy and golden.
5. Serve warm with a dip of your choice.

Nutritional Info: Calories: 180 | Fat: 8g | Carbs: 28g | Protein: 2g

SAUTÉED KALE WITH GARLIC

Prep: 10 mins | Cook: 5 mins | Serves: 4

Ingredients:
- **US:** 300g kale (chopped), 15ml olive oil, 2 cloves garlic (sliced), Salt and pepper to taste
- **UK:** 300g kale (chopped), 15ml olive oil, 2 cloves garlic (sliced), Salt and pepper to taste

Instructions:
1. Heat olive oil in a pan over medium heat.
2. Add garlic and cook for 1 minute until fragrant.
3. Add chopped kale and sauté for 3-4 minutes until wilted.
4. Season with salt and pepper, and serve immediately.

Nutritional Info: Calories: 100 | Fat: 7g | Carbs: 8g | Protein: 3g

CUCUMBER AND TOMATO SALAD

Prep: 10 mins | Cook: 0 mins | Serves: 4

Ingredients:
- **US:** 200g cucumber (sliced), 200g cherry tomatoes (halved), 30g red onion (finely chopped), 30ml olive oil, 15ml red wine vinegar, Salt and pepper to taste
- **UK:** 200g cucumber (sliced), 200g cherry tomatoes (halved), 30g red onion (finely chopped), 30ml olive oil, 15ml red wine vinegar, Salt and pepper to taste

Instructions:
1. In a large bowl, combine cucumber, cherry tomatoes, and red onion.
2. Drizzle with olive oil and red wine vinegar.
3. Season with salt and pepper, then toss gently.
4. Serve immediately or chill until ready to serve.

Nutritional Info: Calories: 90 | Fat: 8g | Carbs: 7g | Protein: 1g

BROWN RICE PILAF

Prep: 10 mins | Cook: 30 mins | Serves: 4
Ingredients:
- **US:** 200g brown rice, 500ml vegetable broth, 1 onion (chopped), 1 carrot (diced), 30ml olive oil, Salt and pepper to taste
- **UK:** 200g brown rice, 500ml vegetable broth, 1 onion (chopped), 1 carrot (diced), 30ml olive oil, Salt and pepper to taste

Instructions:
1. Heat olive oil in a pot and sauté onion and carrot until soft.
2. Add brown rice and stir for 2 minutes.
3. Pour in vegetable broth and bring to a boil.
4. Reduce heat, cover, and simmer for 25-30 minutes until rice is tender.
5. Fluff with a fork and season with salt and pepper.

Nutritional Info: Calories: 220 | Fat: 7g | Carbs: 36g | Protein: 5g

ROASTED BRUSSELS SPROUTS WITH BALSAMIC GLAZE

Prep: 10 mins | Cook: 25 mins | Serves: 4
Ingredients:
- **US:** 300g Brussels sprouts (halved), 30ml olive oil, 30ml balsamic vinegar, 1 tablespoon honey, Salt and pepper to taste
- **UK:** 300g Brussels sprouts (halved), 30ml olive oil, 30ml balsamic vinegar, 1 tablespoon honey, Salt and pepper to taste

Instructions:
1. Preheat your oven to 200°C (180°C fan)/400°F.
2. Toss Brussels sprouts with olive oil, salt, and pepper.
3. Roast for 20-25 minutes until crispy.
4. In a small pan, heat balsamic vinegar and honey until reduced and thickened.
5. Drizzle the glaze over the roasted sprouts before serving.

Nutritional Info: Calories: 180 | Fat: 9g | Carbs: 21g | Protein: 5g

MASHED CAULIFLOWER

Prep: 10 mins | Cook: 15 mins | Serves: 4
Ingredients:
- **US:** 500g cauliflower florets, 30ml milk, 30g butter, Salt and pepper to taste
- **UK:** 500g cauliflower florets, 30ml milk, 30g butter, Salt and pepper to taste

Instructions:
1. Steam cauliflower florets until tender, about 10-15 minutes.
2. Drain and place in a bowl.
3. Mash with a potato masher or blend until smooth.
4. Stir in milk and butter, and season with salt and pepper.
5. Serve warm as a creamy side dish.

Nutritional Info: Calories: 150 | Fat: 9g | Carbs: 12g | Protein: 4g

WHOLE GRAIN COUSCOUS WITH HERBS

Prep: 10 mins | Cook: 10 mins | Serves: 4

Ingredients:
- **US:** 200g whole grain couscous, 250ml water, 30g fresh parsley (chopped), 30g fresh mint (chopped), 15ml olive oil, Salt and pepper to taste
- **UK:** 200g whole grain couscous, 250ml water, 30g fresh parsley (chopped), 30g fresh mint (chopped), 15ml olive oil, Salt and pepper to taste

Instructions:
1. Bring water to a boil and pour over couscous in a bowl. Cover and let steam for 5 minutes.
2. Fluff with a fork and stir in olive oil, parsley, and mint.
3. Season with salt and pepper, and serve warm or at room temperature.

Nutritional Info: Calories: 190 | Fat: 6g | Carbs: 28g | Protein: 6g

SMOOTHIES AND BEVERAGES

GREEN GODDESS SMOOTHIE

Prep: 10 mins | Serves: 2

Ingredients:
- **US:** 150g spinach, 1 small green apple (cored), 1/2 cucumber, 1 ripe banana, 240ml water or unsweetened almond milk, 1 tablespoon chia seeds
- **UK:** 150g spinach, 1 small green apple (cored), 1/2 cucumber, 1 ripe banana, 240ml water or unsweetened almond milk, 1 tablespoon chia seeds

Instructions:
1. Wash the spinach and cucumber thoroughly.
2. Peel and chop the banana and core the apple.
3. Combine all ingredients in a blender, adding water or almond milk.
4. Blend until smooth, adding more liquid if needed for your desired consistency.
5. Pour into glasses and serve immediately.

Nutritional Info: Calories: 180 | Fat: 3g | Carbs: 34g | Protein: 4g

BERRY BLAST SMOOTHIE

Prep: 10 mins | Serves: 2

Ingredients:
- **US:** 150g mixed berries (fresh or frozen), 1 banana, 240ml water or low-fat milk, 1 tablespoon flaxseeds
- **UK:** 150g mixed berries (fresh or frozen), 1 banana, 240ml water or low-fat milk, 1 tablespoon flaxseeds

Instructions:
1. Peel the banana and add it to the blender with the mixed berries.
2. Add water or milk and flaxseeds.
3. Blend until smooth. If the smoothie is too thick, add a bit more liquid.
4. Serve immediately.

Nutritional Info: Calories: 200 | Fat: 2g | Carbs: 45g | Protein: 5g

TROPICAL TURMERIC SMOOTHIE

Prep: 10 mins | Serves: 2

Ingredients:
- **US:** 1/2 cup pineapple chunks, 1/2 cup mango chunks, 1 banana, 240ml coconut water, 1/2 teaspoon ground turmeric
- **UK:** 1/2 cup pineapple chunks, 1/2 cup mango chunks, 1 banana, 240ml coconut water, 1/2 teaspoon ground turmeric

Instructions:
1. Peel and chop the banana, and add it with pineapple and mango to the blender.
2. Pour in coconut water and add ground turmeric.
3. Blend until smooth, adjusting thickness with more coconut water if needed.
4. Serve chilled.

Nutritional Info: Calories: 220 | Fat: 1g | Carbs: 53g | Protein: 2g

PEANUT BUTTER BANANA SHAKE

Prep: 5 mins | Serves: 1

Ingredients:
- **US:** 1 ripe banana, 2 tablespoons natural peanut butter, 240ml skim milk, 1 teaspoon honey (optional)
- **UK:** 1 ripe banana, 2 tablespoons natural peanut butter, 240ml skim milk, 1 teaspoon honey (optional)

Instructions:
1. Peel and slice the banana.
2. Combine banana, peanut butter, and milk in a blender.
3. Blend until smooth. Add honey if desired for extra sweetness.
4. Pour into a glass and enjoy.

Nutritional Info: Calories: 290 | Fat: 12g | Carbs: 35g | Protein: 11g

WATERMELON MINT COOLER

Prep: 10 mins | Serves: 2

Ingredients:
- **US:** 2 cups watermelon chunks, 1/4 cup fresh mint leaves, 240ml sparkling water, 1 tablespoon lime juice
- **UK:** 2 cups watermelon chunks, 1/4 cup fresh mint leaves, 240ml sparkling water, 1 tablespoon lime juice

Instructions:
1. Blend the watermelon chunks until smooth.
2. Strain through a sieve into a jug to remove pulp.
3. Add mint leaves and lime juice, stirring well.
4. Top with sparkling water and serve chilled.

Nutritional Info: Calories: 120 | Fat: 0g | Carbs: 30g | Protein: 1g

GOLDEN MILK (TURMERIC LATTE)

Prep: 5 mins | Cook: 5 mins | Serves: 2

Ingredients:
- **US:** 2 cups almond milk, 1/2 teaspoon ground turmeric, 1/2 teaspoon ground cinnamon, 1 tablespoon honey
- **UK:** 2 cups almond milk, 1/2 teaspoon ground turmeric, 1/2 teaspoon ground cinnamon, 1 tablespoon honey

Instructions:
1. Heat almond milk in a saucepan over medium heat.
2. Whisk in turmeric, cinnamon, and honey.
3. Heat until steaming, but do not boil.
4. Pour into mugs and serve warm.

Nutritional Info: Calories: 100 | Fat: 2g | Carbs: 18g | Protein: 2g

CUCUMBER LEMON WATER

Prep: 10 mins | Serves: 4

Ingredients:
- **US:** 1 cucumber (sliced), 1 lemon (sliced), 1 liter water
- **UK:** 1 cucumber (sliced), 1 lemon (sliced), 1 liter water

Instructions:
1. Slice the cucumber and lemon thinly.
2. Add slices to a jug of water.
3. Let infuse in the fridge for at least 1 hour before serving.
4. Serve chilled, with ice if desired.

Nutritional Info: Calories: 10 | Fat: 0g | Carbs: 2g | Protein: 0g

CHAMOMILE AND LAVENDER TEA

Prep: 5 mins | Steep: 10 mins | Serves: 2

Ingredients:
- **US:** 2 chamomile tea bags, 1 teaspoon dried lavender, 240ml boiling water
- **UK:** 2 chamomile tea bags, 1 teaspoon dried lavender, 240ml boiling water

Instructions:
1. Place the tea bags and dried lavender in a teapot or cup.
2. Pour boiling water over the tea bags and lavender.
3. Let steep for 10 minutes.
4. Remove tea bags and strain out lavender before serving.

Nutritional Info: Calories: 0 | Fat: 0g | Carbs: 0g | Protein: 0g

CARROT AND GINGER JUICE

Prep: 10 mins | Serves: 2

Ingredients:
- **US:** 4 large carrots (peeled), 1 small piece of fresh ginger (about 2cm), 240ml water
- **UK:** 4 large carrots (peeled), 1 small piece of fresh ginger (about 2cm), 240ml water

Instructions:
1. Peel and chop carrots. Peel the ginger.
2. Juice carrots and ginger together using a juicer.
3. Add water to the juice and stir well.
4. Serve immediately, over ice if preferred.

Nutritional Info: Calories: 150 | Fat: 0g | Carbs: 36g | Protein: 2g

PROBIOTIC KEFIR DRINK

Prep: 2 mins | Serves: 1

Ingredients:
- **US:** 240ml kefir, 1/2 cup fresh fruit (optional), 1 teaspoon honey (optional)
- **UK:** 240ml kefir, 1/2 cup fresh fruit (optional), 1 teaspoon honey (optional)

Instructions:
1. Pour kefir into a glass.
2. Add fresh fruit and honey if desired.
3. Stir well and enjoy.

Nutritional Info: Calories: 150 | Fat: 3g | Carbs: 12g | Protein: 8g

SNACKS AND LIGHT BITES

BAKED VEGETABLE CRISPS

Prep: 10 mins | Cook: 20 mins | Serves: 4

Ingredients:
- **US:** 300g mixed vegetables (e.g., carrots, zucchini, sweet potatoes), 15ml olive oil, 1/2 teaspoon paprika, 1/2 teaspoon garlic powder, salt to taste
- **UK:** 300g mixed vegetables (e.g., carrots, courgette, sweet potatoes), 15ml olive oil, 1/2 teaspoon paprika, 1/2 teaspoon garlic powder, salt to taste

Instructions:
1. Preheat your oven to 180°C (350°F). Line a baking tray with parchment paper.
2. Thinly slice the vegetables using a mandolin or sharp knife. The thinner the slices, the crispier the chips.
3. Toss the vegetable slices in a bowl with olive oil, paprika, garlic powder, and salt until evenly coated.
4. Arrange the slices in a single layer on the prepared baking tray.
5. Bake for 15-20 minutes, flipping halfway through, until the edges are crisp and golden.
6. Let the crisps cool on a wire rack to maintain their crunch.
7. Enjoy your homemade vegetable crisps as a light, satisfying snack!

Nutritional Info: Calories: 80 | Fat: 4g | Carbs: 10g | Protein: 1g

HOMEMADE GRANOLA BARS

Prep: 10 mins | Cook: 25 mins | Serves: 8 bars

Ingredients:
- **US:** 200g oats, 100g chopped nuts (e.g., almonds, walnuts), 100g dried fruit (e.g., raisins, cranberries), 60ml honey, 30ml coconut oil
- **UK:** 200g oats, 100g chopped nuts (e.g., almonds, walnuts), 100g dried fruit (e.g., raisins, cranberries), 60ml honey, 30ml coconut oil

Instructions:
1. Preheat your oven to 180°C (350°F). Line a baking tin with parchment paper.
2. In a large bowl, mix the oats, chopped nuts, and dried fruit.
3. In a small saucepan over low heat, warm the honey and coconut oil until melted and combined.
4. Pour the honey mixture over the dry ingredients and stir until everything is evenly coated.
5. Press the mixture firmly into the lined baking tin.
6. Bake for 20-25 minutes, or until the edges are golden brown.
7. Let cool completely before cutting into bars.
8. Store in an airtight container for a quick, nutritious snack.

Nutritional Info: Calories: 150 | Fat: 7g | Carbs: 20g | Protein: 4g

WHOLE GRAIN CRACKERS WITH HUMMUS

Prep: 5 mins | Cook: 10 mins | Serves: 4

Ingredients:
- **US:** 100g whole grain crackers, 150g hummus (store-bought or homemade)
- **UK:** 100g whole grain crackers, 150g hummus (store-bought or homemade)

Instructions:
1. Arrange the whole grain crackers on a serving plate.
2. Scoop the hummus into a small bowl and place it next to the crackers.
3. Serve as a light, crunchy snack with a side of creamy hummus.

Nutritional Info: Calories: 120 | Fat: 5g | Carbs: 15g | Protein: 4g

APPLE SLICES WITH ALMOND BUTTER

Prep: 5 mins | Cook: 0 mins | Serves: 2
Ingredients:
- **US:** 2 medium apples, sliced, 60g almond butter
- **UK:** 2 medium apples, sliced, 60g almond butter

Instructions:
1. Wash and core the apples, then slice them into thin wedges.
2. Serve the apple slices with a dollop of almond butter for dipping.

Nutritional Info: Calories: 200 | Fat: 12g | Carbs: 22g | Protein: 6g

ROASTED CHICKPEAS

Prep: 10 mins | Cook: 30 mins | Serves: 4
Ingredients:
- **US:** 400g canned chickpeas (drained and rinsed), 15ml olive oil, 1/2 teaspoon cumin, 1/2 teaspoon paprika, salt to taste
- **UK:** 400g canned chickpeas (drained and rinsed), 15ml olive oil, 1/2 teaspoon cumin, 1/2 teaspoon paprika, salt to taste

Instructions:
1. Preheat your oven to 200°C (400°F). Line a baking tray with parchment paper.
2. Pat the chickpeas dry with a paper towel.
3. Toss the chickpeas in a bowl with olive oil, cumin, paprika, and salt.
4. Spread the chickpeas in a single layer on the prepared baking tray.
5. Roast for 25-30 minutes, shaking the tray occasionally, until the chickpeas are crispy.
6. Let cool slightly before enjoying as a crunchy snack.

Nutritional Info: Calories: 120 | Fat: 5g | Carbs: 18g | Protein: 6g

GREEK YOGURT WITH BERRIES AND HONEY

Prep: 5 mins | Cook: 0 mins | Serves: 2
Ingredients:
- **US:** 250g Greek yogurt, 100g mixed berries, 1 tablespoon honey
- **UK:** 250g Greek yogurt, 100g mixed berries, 1 tablespoon honey

Instructions:
1. Spoon the Greek yogurt into serving bowls.
2. Top with mixed berries and drizzle with honey.
3. Serve immediately for a refreshing, protein-packed snack.

Nutritional Info: Calories: 180 | Fat: 2g | Carbs: 24g | Protein: 12g

VEGETABLE STICKS WITH TZATZIKI DIP

Prep: 10 mins | Cook: 0 mins | Serves: 4
Ingredients:
- **US:** 200g mixed vegetable sticks (e.g., cucumber, carrot, bell pepper), 150g tzatziki dip
- **UK:** 200g mixed vegetable sticks (e.g., cucumber, carrot, bell pepper), 150g tzatziki dip

Instructions:
1. Arrange the vegetable sticks on a platter.
2. Serve with a bowl of tzatziki dip for dipping.
3. Enjoy this light and refreshing snack that's full of flavour.

Nutritional Info: Calories: 70 | Fat: 3g | Carbs: 9g | Protein: 2g

BAKED KALE CHIPS

Prep: 10 mins | Cook: 15 mins | Serves: 4

Ingredients:
- **US:** 200g kale leaves, 15ml olive oil, 1/2 teaspoon sea salt
- **UK:** 200g kale leaves, 15ml olive oil, 1/2 teaspoon sea salt

Instructions:
1. Preheat your oven to 160°C (320°F). Line a baking tray with parchment paper.
2. Remove the kale leaves from the stems and tear into bite-sized pieces.
3. Toss the kale with olive oil and sea salt until evenly coated.
4. Spread the kale in a single layer on the baking tray.
5. Bake for 10-15 minutes, or until crispy, checking frequently to prevent burning.
6. Let cool before serving.

Nutritional Info: Calories: 80 | Fat: 6g | Carbs: 8g | Protein: 2g

WHOLE GRAIN MUFFINS WITH FRUIT

Prep: 15 mins | Cook: 25 mins | Serves: 12 muffins

Ingredients:
- **US:** 250g whole grain flour, 100g fresh fruit (e.g., blueberries, diced apple), 100g honey, 2 eggs, 60ml milk
- **UK:** 250g whole grain flour, 100g fresh fruit (e.g., blueberries, diced apple), 100g honey, 2 eggs, 60ml milk

Instructions:
1. Preheat your oven to 180°C (350°F). Line a muffin tin with paper liners.
2. In a bowl, mix the flour and honey together.
3. In another bowl, whisk the eggs and milk.
4. Combine the wet and dry ingredients, then fold in the fresh fruit.
5. Divide the batter evenly among the muffin cups.
6. Bake for 20-25 minutes, or until a skewer inserted into the centre comes out clean.
7. Cool before serving.

Nutritional Info: Calories: 150 | Fat: 5g | Carbs: 22g | Protein: 4g

HOMEMADE TRAIL MIX

Prep: 5 mins | Cook: 0 mins | Serves: 4

Ingredients:
- **US:** 100g mixed nuts (e.g., almonds, walnuts), 50g dried fruit (e.g., raisins, apricots), 30g sunflower seeds, 30g pumpkin seeds, 1/2 teaspoon cinnamon (optional)
- **UK:** 100g mixed nuts (e.g., almonds, walnuts), 50g dried fruit (e.g., raisins, apricots), 30g sunflower seeds, 30g pumpkin seeds, 1/2 teaspoon cinnamon (optional)

Instructions:
1. In a large bowl, combine the mixed nuts, dried fruit, sunflower seeds, and pumpkin seeds.
2. If using, sprinkle with cinnamon and mix well.
3. Portion into individual snack bags or airtight containers for easy grab-and-go snacks.
4. Store in a cool, dry place.

Nutritional Info: Calories: 180 | Fat: 12g | Carbs: 15g | Protein: 6g

DESSERTS

DARK CHOCOLATE AVOCADO MOUSSE

Prep: 10 mins | Cook: 0 mins | Serves: 4

Ingredients:
- **US:** 2 ripe avocados, 60g dark chocolate (melted), 30ml honey, 1 teaspoon vanilla extract
- **UK:** 2 ripe avocados, 60g dark chocolate (melted), 30ml honey, 1 teaspoon vanilla extract

Instructions:
1. Scoop the avocado flesh into a blender.
2. Add melted chocolate, honey, and vanilla extract.
3. Blend until smooth and creamy.
4. Chill in the fridge for at least 30 minutes before serving.

Nutritional Info: Calories: 250 | Fat: 18g | Carbs: 20g | Protein: 3g

ALMOND AND DATE ENERGY BALLS

Prep: 15 mins | Cook: 0 mins | Serves: 12 balls

Ingredients:
- **US:** 150g dates, 100g almonds, 1 tablespoon chia seeds, 1 tablespoon unsweetened cocoa powder
- **UK:** 150g dates, 100g almonds, 1 tablespoon chia seeds, 1 tablespoon unsweetened cocoa powder

Instructions:
1. In a food processor, pulse dates and almonds until finely chopped.
2. Add chia seeds and cocoa powder, then pulse until combined.
3. Roll mixture into small balls and refrigerate until firm.

Nutritional Info: Calories: 100 per ball | Fat: 6g | Carbs: 12g | Protein: 2g

CHIA SEED PUDDING WITH BERRIES

Prep: 5 mins | Cook: 0 mins | Serves: 4

Ingredients:
- **US:** 60g chia seeds, 240ml almond milk, 30ml honey, 100g mixed berries
- **UK:** 60g chia seeds, 240ml almond milk, 30ml honey, 100g mixed berries

Instructions:
1. In a bowl, whisk together chia seeds, almond milk, and honey.
2. Cover and refrigerate for at least 4 hours or overnight.
3. Stir well before serving and top with mixed berries.

Nutritional Info: Calories: 220 | Fat: 9g | Carbs: 28g | Protein: 6g

BANANA "NICE" CREAM

Prep: 10 mins | Cook: 0 mins | Serves: 2

Ingredients:
- **US:** 2 ripe bananas, 30ml almond milk, 1/2 teaspoon vanilla extract
- **UK:** 2 ripe bananas, 30ml almond milk, 1/2 teaspoon vanilla extract

Instructions:
1. Peel and slice the bananas, then freeze the slices.
2. Blend the frozen banana slices with almond milk and vanilla extract until smooth.
3. Serve immediately as a creamy, dairy-free ice cream.

Nutritional Info: Calories: 160 | Fat: 0g | Carbs: 42g | Protein: 1g

WHOLE GRAIN OATMEAL COOKIES

Prep: 15 mins | Cook: 15 mins | Serves: 12 cookies

Ingredients:
- **US:** 120g whole grain oats, 60g whole wheat flour, 50g honey, 30ml olive oil, 1 teaspoon vanilla extract, 1/2 teaspoon baking soda
- **UK:** 120g whole grain oats, 60g whole wheat flour, 50g honey, 30ml olive oil, 1 teaspoon vanilla extract, 1/2 teaspoon baking soda

Instructions:
1. Preheat your oven to 180°C (350°F) and line a baking sheet with parchment paper.
2. In a bowl, mix oats, flour, baking soda, and honey.
3. Stir in olive oil and vanilla extract until well combined.
4. Scoop spoonfuls of dough onto the baking sheet and flatten slightly.
5. Bake for 12-15 minutes or until golden brown.
6. Let cool before serving.

Nutritional Info: Calories: 120 per cookie | Fat: 5g | Carbs: 16g | Protein: 2g

POACHED PEARS IN SPICED TEA

Prep: 10 mins | Cook: 30 mins | Serves: 4

Ingredients:
- **US:** 4 ripe pears, 500ml black tea, 60ml honey, 1 cinnamon stick, 2 cloves
- **UK:** 4 ripe pears, 500ml black tea, 60ml honey, 1 cinnamon stick, 2 cloves

Instructions:
1. Peel and core the pears, leaving the stems on.
2. In a saucepan, combine black tea, honey, cinnamon stick, and cloves. Bring to a simmer.
3. Add pears and simmer gently for 20-30 minutes until tender.
4. Remove pears and let cool. Reduce the liquid if needed to make a syrup.
5. Serve pears with a drizzle of the spiced syrup.

Nutritional Info: Calories: 140 | Fat: 0g | Carbs: 36g | Protein: 1g

BAKED APPLES WITH CINNAMON

Prep: 10 mins | Cook: 25 mins | Serves: 4

Ingredients:
- **US:** 4 medium apples, 30ml honey, 1 teaspoon ground cinnamon, 1/4 teaspoon nutmeg, 20g chopped walnuts (optional)
- **UK:** 4 medium apples, 30ml honey, 1 teaspoon ground cinnamon, 1/4 teaspoon nutmeg, 20g chopped walnuts (optional)

Instructions:
1. Preheat your oven to 180°C (350°F).
2. Core the apples and place them in a baking dish.
3. In a small bowl, mix honey, cinnamon, and nutmeg. Drizzle this mixture over the apples.
4. If using, sprinkle the chopped walnuts on top.
5. Bake for 20-25 minutes until the apples are tender.
6. Serve warm, optionally with a dollop of Greek yogurt.

Nutritional Info: Calories: 150 | Fat: 2g | Carbs: 36g | Protein: 1g

GREEK YOGURT PANNA COTTA

Prep: 15 mins | Cook: 5 mins | Serves: 4

Ingredients:
- **US:** 300ml Greek yogurt, 200ml milk, 50g honey, 1 packet (7g) gelatin, 1 teaspoon vanilla extract
- **UK:** 300ml Greek yogurt, 200ml milk, 50g honey, 1 packet (7g) gelatin, 1 teaspoon vanilla extract

Instructions:
1. In a small saucepan, heat milk and honey until warm but not boiling.
2. Dissolve gelatin in a little cold water, then stir into the warm milk mixture.
3. Remove from heat and stir in Greek yogurt and vanilla extract.
4. Pour into serving glasses and refrigerate for at least 4 hours until set.
5. Serve chilled, optionally topped with a berry compote.

Nutritional Info: Calories: 180 | Fat: 5g | Carbs: 24g | Protein: 8g

FRUIT SALAD WITH MINT AND LIME

Prep: 10 mins | Cook: 0 mins | Serves: 4

Ingredients:
- **US:** 200g watermelon, 150g strawberries, 1 ripe kiwi, 1 lime (juiced), 1 tablespoon fresh mint leaves (chopped)
- **UK:** 200g watermelon, 150g strawberries, 1 ripe kiwi, 1 lime (juiced), 1 tablespoon fresh mint leaves (chopped)

Instructions:
1. Cut the watermelon into bite-sized cubes and slice the strawberries.
2. Peel and slice the kiwi.
3. In a bowl, combine all the fruit.
4. Drizzle with lime juice and sprinkle with chopped mint leaves.
5. Toss gently to combine and serve immediately.

Nutritional Info: Calories: 80 | Fat: 0g | Carbs: 20g | Protein: 1g

BERRY CRUMBLE WITH OAT TOPPING

Prep: 10 mins | Cook: 30 mins | Serves: 4

Ingredients:
- **US:** 300g mixed berries (fresh or frozen), 50g honey, 100g whole grain oats, 50g whole wheat flour, 30g unsalted butter
- **UK:** 300g mixed berries (fresh or frozen), 50g honey, 100g whole grain oats, 50g whole wheat flour, 30g unsalted butter

Instructions:
1. Preheat your oven to 180°C (350°F).
2. In a bowl, mix berries with honey and place them in a baking dish.
3. In another bowl, combine oats, flour, and butter. Rub together until the mixture resembles coarse crumbs.
4. Sprinkle the oat mixture over the berries.
5. Bake for 25-30 minutes until the topping is golden and the berries are bubbling.
6. Serve warm or at room temperature.

Nutritional Info: Calories: 220 | Fat: 8g | Carbs: 35g | Protein: 3g

GLOSSARY

Diverticulitis: A condition where small, bulging pouches (diverticula) in the lining of the digestive system become inflamed or infected.

Diverticula: Small, bulging pouches that can form in the lining of the digestive system, most commonly in the colon.

Fiber: A type of carbohydrate that the body can't digest, important for digestive health and managing diverticulitis.

Soluble fiber: A type of fiber that dissolves in water, forming a gel-like substance in the gut.

Insoluble fiber: A type of fiber that doesn't dissolve in water and helps food pass through the digestive system.

Probiotics: Live bacteria and yeasts that are good for digestive health, often found in fermented foods.

Prebiotics: Types of dietary fiber that feed the friendly bacteria in your gut.

Anti-inflammatory: Foods or substances that help reduce inflammation in the body.

Whole grains: Grains that contain all parts of the kernel, including the bran, germ, and endosperm.

Legumes: A family of plants that includes beans, peas, and lentils, which are high in fiber and protein.

Antioxidants: Substances that can prevent or slow damage to cells caused by free radicals.

Phytonutrients: Compounds found in plants that may have health-promoting properties.

Bland diet: A diet of soft, low-fiber foods that are easy to digest, often recommended during flare-ups.

Flare-up: A period when symptoms of diverticulitis worsen.

Remission: A period when symptoms of diverticulitis are reduced or absent.

Low-residue diet: A diet that limits high-fiber foods to reduce the amount of undigested material passing through the large intestine.

FODMAP: Fermentable Oligosaccharides, Disaccharides, Monosaccharides, and Polyols; types of carbohydrates that can be difficult to digest for some people.

Inflammation: The body's response to injury or infection, characterized by redness, swelling, heat, and pain.

Colitis: Inflammation of the inner lining of the colon.

Gut microbiome: The community of microorganisms living in the digestive tract.

Hydration: The process of providing an adequate amount of water to bodily tissues.

Electrolytes: Minerals in the blood and other bodily fluids that carry an electric charge and are important for various bodily functions.

Antispasmodic: A type of medication that helps relieve smooth muscle spasms, particularly in the digestive tract.

Probiotic supplement: A product containing live bacteria intended to maintain or improve the "good" bacteria in the body.

Prebiotic supplement: A product containing substances that induce the growth or activity of beneficial microorganisms.

Gluten: A protein found in wheat, barley, and rye that some people may have difficulty digesting.

Lactose: A type of sugar found in milk and dairy products that some people have difficulty digesting.

Fermentation: The process by which bacteria break down sugars, often used in food preparation to create probiotic-rich foods.

Meal prep: The practice of preparing meals or meal components ahead of time to facilitate healthy eating.

Portion control: The practice of controlling the amount of food consumed in one sitting.

Mindful eating: The practice of being fully attentive to your food as you buy, prepare, serve, and consume it.

60 DAY MEAL PLAN

Day	Breakfast	Lunch	Dinner	Snack/Light Bite
1	Smooth Banana Oat Porridge	Tomato Basil Bisque with Whole Grain Roll	Baked Lemon Herb Chicken with Quinoa	Greek Yogurt with Berries & Honey
2	Apple Cinnamon Overnight Oats	Roasted Red Pepper Hummus with Veggie Sticks	Lentil & Sweet Potato Curry	Baked Kale Chips
3	Chia Seed Pudding with Mango	Tuna and White Bean Salad	Grilled Salmon with Dill Sauce & Veggies	Apple Slices with Almond Butter
4	Spinach and Feta Frittata	Baked Falafel Bites with Cucumber Salad	Black Bean and Sweet Potato Burrito Bowl	Roasted Chickpeas
5	Buckwheat Pancakes with Blueberry Compote	Zucchini and Pea Soup	Baked Chicken Fajitas	Whole Grain Crackers with Hummus
6	Berry Yoghurt Parfait	Chickpea and Spinach Curry	Grilled Portobello Mushroom Steaks	Homemade Granola Bars
7	Scrambled Tofu with Herbs	Carrot and Ginger Soup	Baked Tilapia with Tomato & Olive Topping	Roasted Vegetable Crisps
8	Whole Grain Toast with Avocado Spread	Lentil and Vegetable Broth	Vegetable Lasagna with Whole Grain Pasta	Greek Yogurt with Honey & Almonds
9	Peach and Ginger Smoothie Bowl	Minestrone with Whole Grain Pasta	Grilled Salmon with Steamed Green Beans	Baked Sweet Potato Wedges
10	Vegetable and Cheese Omelette	Quinoa Tabbouleh with Grilled Veggies	Poached Cod with Herb Broth	Baked Apples with Cinnamon
11	Smooth Banana Oat Porridge	Tomato and Lentil Bolognese	Roasted Brussels Sprouts with Balsamic	Fruit Salad with Mint and Lime
12	Spinach and Feta Frittata	Baked Falafel Bites with Cucumber Salad	Turkey Burgers with Avocado Spread	Greek Yogurt with Berries
13	Buckwheat Pancakes with Blueberry Compote	Zucchini and Pea Soup	Grilled Chicken & Vegetable Kebabs	Whole Grain Muffins with Fruit
14	Chia Seed Pudding with Mango	Lentil & Sweet Potato Curry	Grilled Portobello Mushroom Steaks	Homemade Trail Mix
15	Scrambled Tofu with Herbs	Roasted Red Pepper Hummus with Crackers	Black Bean & Sweet Potato Burrito Bowl	Baked Vegetable Crisps

Super Easy Diverticulitis Cookbook

Day	Breakfast	Lunch	Dinner	Snack/Light Bite
16	Whole Grain Toast with Avocado Spread	Carrot and Ginger Soup	Eggplant Parmesan (Baked)	Greek Yogurt with Honey
17	Apple Cinnamon Overnight Oats	Tomato Basil Bisque	Baked Lemon Herb Chicken with Quinoa	Roasted Chickpeas
18	Berry Yoghurt Parfait	Lentil and Vegetable Broth	Grilled Salmon with Dill Sauce	Apple Slices with Almond Butter
19	Peach and Ginger Smoothie Bowl	Chickpea & Spinach Curry	Baked Tilapia with Tomato & Olive Topping	Baked Sweet Potato Wedges
20	Chia Seed Pudding with Mango	Quinoa Tabbouleh with Veggies	Vegetable Lasagna with Whole Grain Pasta	Greek Yogurt with Berries
21	Smooth Banana Oat Porridge	Minestrone with Whole Grain Pasta	Grilled Chicken & Vegetable Kebabs	Roasted Vegetable Crisps
22	Spinach and Feta Frittata	Tomato and Lentil Bolognese	Turkey Burgers with Avocado Spread	Whole Grain Crackers with Hummus
23	Scrambled Tofu with Herbs	Baked Falafel Bites	Black Bean & Sweet Potato Burrito Bowl	Homemade Trail Mix
24	Whole Grain Toast with Avocado Spread	Zucchini & Pea Soup	Poached Cod with Herb Broth	Baked Apples with Cinnamon
25	Berry Yoghurt Parfait	Lentil & Vegetable Broth	Eggplant Parmesan (Baked)	Baked Kale Chips
26	Apple Cinnamon Overnight Oats	Carrot and Ginger Soup	Grilled Portobello Mushroom Steaks	Greek Yogurt with Berries
27	Chia Seed Pudding with Mango	Roasted Red Pepper Hummus with Veggies	Grilled Chicken & Vegetable Kebabs	Baked Sweet Potato Wedges
28	Smooth Banana Oat Porridge	Quinoa Tabbouleh with Grilled Veggies	Turkey Burgers with Avocado Spread	Roasted Chickpeas
29	Spinach and Feta Frittata	Tomato Basil Bisque	Black Bean & Sweet Potato Burrito Bowl	Greek Yogurt with Honey & Almonds
30	Vegetable & Cheese Omelette	Zucchini and Pea Soup	Baked Lemon Herb Chicken with Quinoa	Roasted Vegetable Crisps

Day	Breakfast	Lunch	Dinner	Snack/Light Bite
31	Smooth Banana Oat Porridge	Lentil & Vegetable Broth	Grilled Salmon with Dill Sauce	Apple Slices with Almond Butter
32	Buckwheat Pancakes with Blueberry Compote	Chickpea and Spinach Curry	Baked Tilapia with Tomato & Olive Topping	Greek Yogurt with Berries
33	Chia Seed Pudding with Mango	Quinoa Tabbouleh with Grilled Veggies	Grilled Chicken & Vegetable Kebabs	Homemade Trail Mix
34	Scrambled Tofu with Herbs	Minestrone with Whole Grain Pasta	Eggplant Parmesan (Baked)	Baked Apples with Cinnamon
35	Whole Grain Toast with Avocado Spread	Tomato & Lentil Bolognese	Poached Cod with Herb Broth	Baked Vegetable Crisps
36	Apple Cinnamon Overnight Oats	Roasted Red Pepper Hummus with Crackers	Turkey Burgers with Avocado Spread	Roasted Chickpeas
37	Berry Yoghurt Parfait	Zucchini and Pea Soup	Black Bean & Sweet Potato Burrito Bowl	Greek Yogurt with Honey
38	Peach and Ginger Smoothie Bowl	Carrot and Ginger Soup	Baked Lemon Herb Chicken with Quinoa	Baked Sweet Potato Wedges
39	Chia Seed Pudding with Mango	Lentil and Vegetable Broth	Grilled Salmon with Dill Sauce	Apple Slices with Almond Butter
40	Spinach and Feta Frittata	Chickpea & Spinach Curry	Grilled Chicken & Vegetable Kebabs	Homemade Trail Mix
41	Smooth Banana Oat Porridge	Minestrone with Whole Grain Pasta	Black Bean & Sweet Potato Burrito Bowl	Greek Yogurt with Berries
42	Whole Grain Toast with Avocado Spread	Quinoa Tabbouleh with Grilled Veggies	Poached Cod with Herb Broth	Roasted Vegetable Crisps
43	Scrambled Tofu with Herbs	Tomato & Lentil Bolognese	Turkey Burgers with Avocado Spread	Roasted Chickpeas
44	Buckwheat Pancakes with Blueberry Compote	Zucchini & Pea Soup	Grilled Chicken & Vegetable Kebabs	Greek Yogurt with Berries
45	Peach and Ginger Smoothie Bowl	Lentil & Vegetable Broth	Baked Lemon Herb Chicken with Quinoa	Baked Sweet Potato Wedges

Day	Breakfast	Lunch	Dinner	Snack/Light Bite
46	Spinach and Feta Frittata	Tomato Basil Bisque	Grilled Salmon with Dill Sauce	Apple Slices with Almond Butter
47	Vegetable & Cheese Omelette	Roasted Red Pepper Hummus with Crackers	Black Bean & Sweet Potato Burrito Bowl	Baked Vegetable Crisps
48	Smooth Banana Oat Porridge	Minestrone with Whole Grain Pasta	Baked Tilapia with Tomato & Olive Topping	Greek Yogurt with Honey
49	Chia Seed Pudding with Mango	Quinoa Tabbouleh with Grilled Veggies	Grilled Chicken & Vegetable Kebabs	Homemade Trail Mix
50	Apple Cinnamon Overnight Oats	Carrot and Ginger Soup	Eggplant Parmesan (Baked)	Roasted Chickpeas
51	Whole Grain Toast with Avocado Spread	Lentil & Vegetable Broth	Baked Lemon Herb Chicken with Quinoa	Greek Yogurt with Berries
52	Spinach and Feta Frittata	Chickpea and Spinach Curry	Black Bean & Sweet Potato Burrito Bowl	Baked Sweet Potato Wedges
53	Smooth Banana Oat Porridge	Roasted Red Pepper Hummus with Veggie Sticks	Grilled Salmon with Dill Sauce	Apple Slices with Almond Butter
54	Chia Seed Pudding with Mango	Zucchini & Pea Soup	Turkey Burgers with Avocado Spread	Greek Yogurt with Honey
55	Buckwheat Pancakes with Blueberry Compote	Tomato Basil Bisque	Poached Cod with Herb Broth	Roasted Vegetable Crisps
56	Scrambled Tofu with Herbs	Lentil & Vegetable Broth	Grilled Chicken & Vegetable Kebabs	Baked Apples with Cinnamon
57	Peach and Ginger Smoothie Bowl	Tomato & Lentil Bolognese	Baked Tilapia with Tomato & Olive Topping	Homemade Trail Mix
58	Whole Grain Toast with Avocado Spread	Minestrone with Whole Grain Pasta	Grilled Salmon with Dill Sauce	Baked Sweet Potato Wedges
59	Smooth Banana Oat Porridge	Roasted Red Pepper Hummus with Veggie Sticks	Black Bean & Sweet Potato Burrito Bowl	Roasted Chickpeas
60	Spinach and Feta Frittata	Zucchini & Pea Soup	Eggplant Parmesan (Baked)	Greek Yogurt with Berries

This meal plan incorporates a balance of protein, fiber, and anti-inflammatory ingredients, tailored to be gentle on the digestive system while offering variety and nutritional value.

CONCLUSION

Living with diverticulitis can be challenging, but with the right approach to diet and lifestyle, it's possible to manage symptoms effectively and improve your overall quality of life. Throughout this book, we've explored the intricacies of diverticulitis, its causes, symptoms, and most importantly, how to navigate your diet to minimize flare-ups and promote digestive health.

We began by understanding diverticulitis and its impact on the digestive system. Armed with this knowledge, we delved into the foundations of a diverticulitis-friendly diet, emphasizing the importance of fiber, hydration, and balanced nutrition. The cooking techniques and tips we've shared are designed to make your culinary journey both enjoyable and beneficial to your health.

The diverse range of recipes provided in this book demonstrates that a diverticulitis-friendly diet doesn't have to be bland or restrictive. From nourishing breakfasts to comforting soups, satisfying main courses, and even delightful desserts, you now have a repertoire of dishes that are not only delicious but also gentle on your digestive system. These recipes prove that you can still enjoy a wide variety of flavors and textures while adhering to your dietary needs.

Remember, the key to success with any diet is consistency and patience. The 30-day meal plan we've included offers a structured approach to incorporating these recipes into your daily life, making it easier to adopt and maintain healthy eating habits. As you progress, you'll likely find that these meals become a natural part of your routine, supporting your digestive health without feeling like a chore.

It's important to note that while diet plays a crucial role in managing diverticulitis, it's just one piece of the puzzle. Regular exercise, stress management, and adequate sleep all contribute to overall digestive health and well-being. We encourage you to work with your healthcare provider to develop a comprehensive plan that addresses all aspects of your health.

As you embark on this journey, be kind to yourself. Changes in diet and lifestyle take time to show results, and there may be setbacks along the way. What matters most is your commitment to your health and your willingness to make positive changes. Celebrate small victories and don't be discouraged by temporary setbacks.

We hope that this book serves as a valuable resource in your journey towards better digestive health. The recipes, tips, and information provided here are designed to empower you with the knowledge and tools needed to take control of your diet and, by extension, your diverticulitis symptoms.

Remember, you're not alone in this journey. Many others are navigating similar challenges, and there are numerous support resources available, including support groups, online communities, and healthcare professionals specializing in digestive health.

As you close this book, we hope you feel inspired and equipped to make positive changes in your diet and lifestyle. Your journey to better digestive health starts now, armed with delicious recipes, practical knowledge, and a renewed sense of empowerment. Here's to your health, happiness, and many enjoyable, nourishing meals ahead!

Printed in Great Britain
by Amazon